NORWAY

Sogne fjord

Hardanger fjord

SWEDEN

Bergen

ICELAND

Reykjavik

Westman Islands

FAEROE ISLANDS

SHETLAND

DENMARK

NORTH SEA

NETHERLANDS

SCOTLAND

North Atlantic Ocean

DOVER STRAIT

ENGLAND

IRELAND

WALES

Cowes

ENGLISH CHANNEL

FRANCE

SPAIN

AZORES

AFRICA

TOPSAIL & BATTLEAXE

"HIRTA"

TOPSAIL & BATTLEAXE

A voyage in the wake of the Vikings

Tom Cunliffe

DAVID & CHARLES
Newton Abbot   London

Maps by Ethan A. Danielson

British Library Cataloguing in Publication Data

Cunliffe, Tom
  Topsail and battleaxe: a voyage in the
  wake of the Vikings.
  1. Voyages and travels——1951–
  2. Seafaring life   3. North Atlantic
  Ocean
  910'.091631   G540

  ISBN 0-7153-9123-2

Phototypeset by Typesetters (Birmingham) Ltd,
Smethwick, West Midlands
and printed in Hong Kong
by South China Printing Co
for David & Charles Publishers plc
Brunel House   Newton Abbot   Devon

Contents

The author at the helm

A good reason for going

MIKE came scrambling aft along the steeply canted deck. It was 3.00am on an early August morning. There was ice in his eyebrows. His bare feet gripped well enough, but there was a blueness about them that would have done little to reassure his mother, if she could have seen him. Fog swirled past the bowsprit as *Hirta* smashed into a wave sending freezing spray ripping across the foredeck like shrapnel. Mike sank gratefully into the cockpit and made the classic 'after you' gesture to Patrick who was clambering out onto the streaming deck, with an expression like an infantryman going over the top.

'Lovely morning for a shower,' he remarked in his deceptively gentle Caithness lilt, to no-one in particular. Then he struggled off to the bow to take over the look-out, his red oilskins merging with the double-reefed staysail, as *Hirta* drove on through the mist.

As Mike scuttled away to steam in his bunk beside the stove, Chris climbed out of the companionway to relieve me at the helm. He was improbably clad in a borrowed oilskin that I'd found in a lost property auction, a ferreting cap a drunk had kicked onto the deck in the Faeroe Islands, and a pair of oversize black farming wellies. He peered myopically at the compass through the water droplets on his John Lennon glasses.

'It's getting like Piccadilly Circus in this cockpit,' he began conversationally, as he eased the wheel a few spokes. 'There's bodies going in all direct . . .' but he got no further. *Hirta* started to come upright as she swung into the wind. The jib and staysail thundered their protest from forward, and the ship was punched almost to a standstill as her bow scooped in a big grey sea. There was a howl of rage from Patrick as his wellies filled with the stone-cold water, followed by a torrent of finest Scots abuse that he could only have picked up during his career in the army. Chris missed little of it as he wound the wheel frantically to leeward. The boat bore thankfully away and settled once more to her task of hammering down to the south-west. Chris hunkered into the collar of his jacket and Patrick returned to squinting at the horizon fifty yards away.

Somewhere far ahead lay the sunshine of the North American summer. Astern lay Cape Farewell and the icebound coast of Greenland, but between us and our destination there was a strong likelihood of drifting bergs coming down on the Labrador Current from Baffin Bay. Right now, for the first time in over a week, we had a wind that enabled us to point in the direction we wanted. *Hirta* was logging 6 knots through an evil sea, but we let her go despite the danger of ice because there was little night at 58°N. Then came the fog. *Hirta* after seventy-five years, was still as innocent of the luxury of radar as she was on her launching day, but with a useable wind after days of frustrating beating we weren't about to waste our chance. We pressed on, with the look-out studying the windswept half-light for the first glimpse of a growler awash in our path. Or even an iceberg.

Leaving Chris steering full and by, I homed in on the galley to brew up. Mike was already snoring; his dark hair dripped onto the wet cabin sole and his nineteen-year-old face looked boyish in the grey dawn light. That was pure deception; Mike was as tough as nails. On the downhill saloon berth my mate, John, opened a bloodshot eye, then shut it a millisecond too late as a deck leak caught it square on. A veteran of many a lash-up, John has suffered such minor aggravations stoically for years.

'How's it going, Skip?' he enquired softly. Before I could answer he added, 'did we get headed again?' He was referring to the fearful racket of blocks and ropes crashing on the deck as the boat had come into the wind a couple of minutes earlier. Evidently the noise had masked Patrick's comments from the sleepers, otherwise he wouldn't have had to ask. After reassurance that the wind was still fair, he went straight back to sleep, determined to grab every second of delight from his hour in the sack. Another drip fell into his beard, but this one didn't disturb him.

In the girls' cabin, my four-year-old daughter was dreaming peacefully, her blonde thatch spilling over her leeboard. The ship could stand on her stern and Hannah wouldn't budge. In the bottom bunk, gently illuminated by the night light, her mother was crashed out under a heap of blankets. Ros managed the whole lurching nightmare of the below-decks operation of the ship, including Hannah, and still contrived to imply, at least most of the time, that she wouldn't ask to be anywhere else.

For the remainder of us, a spell in a Gothic dungeon would have seemed a light-hearted alternative to our present circumstances. The odd thing was that we were all there of our own free will. Unlike many a mariner finding himself in similar straits, none of us had been slipped the Queen's shilling by a crafty press-gang petty officer and, as far as I could tell, no-one was on the run from alternatives so unspeakable that even a bout with the Greenland Sea seemed preferable.

Ros and I owned the boat and so our motivation was the primary driving force of the voyage. Each of the four men who had joined with us in the enterprise had his own reasons for being there. Only Hannah was having the experience thrust upon her, whether she liked it or not. That's the trouble with being four years old – you have to tolerate your parents' lunacies. The one consolation is that, unlike the adults, you don't have to pretend to like it. Fortunately for all of us, Hannah had adapted to life in a small sailing vessel beating leakily to windward in the way that only a child can. She made a snug nest in her cabin and accepted each new day with equanimity, no matter how the ocean dealt the cards.

For years, Ros and I had been fascinated by the medieval Norse and their voyaging. Every schoolboy has thrilled to tales of the Viking scourge and the mighty bearded warriors who held Europe in terror for two hundred years; of the dragon ships rowing up-river out of the dawn with bulwarks of shields, oars flashing in the early sun, and the blood-chilling howls of the berserks as they were unleashed on the cowering monks of the fat Celtic monasteries.

But for the Norsemen it wasn't all beer and skittles. Their voyaging began infamously with summer jaunts to the south on the 'rape and pillage run', but in time social and economic pressures steered them towards sterner passages across the Western Ocean. After taking over the Atlantic islands of Orkney, Shetland and the Faeroes, they had established a thriving colony in Iceland by the year AD900. From there they set up a sound beach-head in south-west Greenland and not long afterwards an enterprising band of fortune hunters landed in North America, a few years before AD1000.

When we decided to sail in *Hirta* to the United States a millenium later the question naturally arose as to which route to take. For vessels bound under sail towards New England from Old England there are three main possibilities.

The first is the 'milk run' which makes use of the north-east trade winds in the Tropics and provides a logical and easy means of sailing across the Atlantic. It does, however, involve an uninterrupted passage of over a month from, say, the Canary Islands, to a landfall in the States.

The second route is officially designated the 'low-powered steamer route'. Here the boat makes the best way she can across the gentler latitudes between the trade winds and the great west winds that blow north of the fortieth parallel. Down to the Azores, across to Bermuda, then north-west to home. The passages are shorter, but headwinds are a possibility at any time and lack of wind is likely to be a problem.

The third passage known to sailors as the 'northern route' passes north of the Great Circle, which is the most direct line from Europe to New England. As she follows this track the vessel traverses north of the Gulf Stream and north of the centres of the depressions which generate the North Atlantic westerly winds. This gives her a chance of some easterlies to help her on her

(overleaf) Ros and Hannah enjoying a windless day in
the Norwegian fjords

13

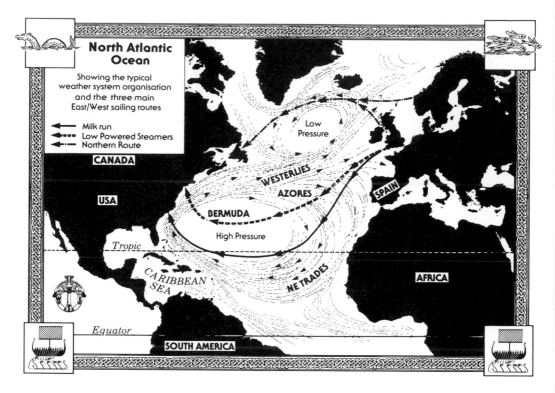

Typical weather system organisation and three main east-west sailing routes in the North Atlantic

way. In these latitudes the currents are fairly slack and tend, in general, to favour a westbound ship. So it's not as bad as it looks. In theory.

A thousand years ago the Viking seafarers from Norway were making their westing in the Atlantic by using these prevailing northern conditions. Nobody told them that the wind blows in an anticlockwise spiral around a low pressure system and that if they kept well up this would give them a good percentage of easterlies, but experience taught them that it was so.

The Vikings were, by nature, coastal navigators although they were well able to handle short passages out of sight of land. The longest hop on their route to America from Norway is only about six hundred miles and if they were prepared to deviate a little from the direct compass courses the distances between landfalls could be made even less. Furthermore in high summer, for most of the passage, there would be no darkness to hide their seamarks, though this, as we shall see, was a mixed blessing.

The idea of sailing to America following the ancient route of the Norsemen had plenty to commend it to us. The easterly winds would be a

16

delight. Endless daylight means no night watches; no pulling reefs down in the usual thick darkness, no burning up battery power and subsequent tiresome running of engines to recharge. In fact, the removal at a stroke of many of the nastier elements of seafaring. The short passages would maintain everyone's interest, particularly Hannah's, and we could enjoy frequent runs ashore at the ancient Norse ocean staging posts. It looked as though the Vikings got it right. America by the coastal route. That was for us.

Our interest in Norse voyaging now grew rapidly and we scoured the libraries of England for translations of the Icelandic Sagas and commentaries on them.

The sagas form one of the major sources of information about this period of northern history. The folk who star in them were far too busy getting on with the business of life and the dealing of death to bother with such unmanly pursuits as reading and writing, so their deeds of fame and villainy passed down initially through the spoken word. In order to ensure that future generations saw things in the right light, it was customary to report such matters in a formal manner, often in verse. Most families who fancied their social position would employ a *skald* whose job it was to create and remember these epics and to repeat them when called upon to do so.

Because there were no surnames as we know them, and a nobleman's ancestry was of the highest importance to him, genealogies are often related in the sagas. The necessity for accuracy in this encouraged a *skald* to develop clarity of memory, for it was a fine social boost for his boss to be able to brag of descent from the likes of Hraerek the Ringscatterer, or the awful Eirik Bloodaxe.

The sagas were written down for the first time around the twelfth century and the versions available to us are generally taken from a second or third transcription. This means that the Chinese-whisper effect is kept within the bounds of reason. Different versions of the same event, however, often vary enough to keep scholars on their toes and give an ordinary sailor plenty to wonder about. For him, the delight of saga reading is not in a toothcomb analysis of all the historical possibilities, but in enjoyment of the characters and events. Sometimes a writer will tell us nothing directly about a person, but will give us enough circumstantial detail about his actions for us to formulate a clear picture.

On other occasions there will be a bald statement of a person's character. Delightful remarks like '. . . there was little chance of meeting anyone worse after meeting him', are not uncommon. (From *Njal's Saga* by Magnus Magnusson and Hermann Pálsson)

The story of the family which formed the spearhead of the Viking push to

(overleaf) This is what sailing is all about

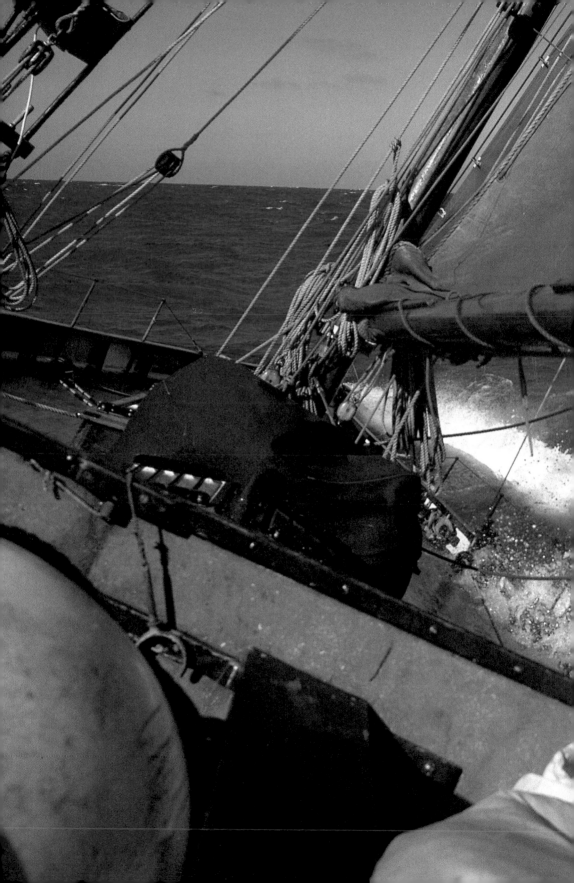

Greenland and then ultimately to America begins in Norway. After some difficulties at home, they move to Iceland where the old man dies and his son, Eirik the Red, takes charge. Eirik's fate leads him to Greenland and it is from there that his own son, Leif, becomes the first documented European to set foot in the New World. Precisely where Leif Eirikson landed will always be the subject of scholastic controversy but there is a powerful argument in favour of Newfoundland or Labrador. There is also an excavated archeological site at l'Anse aux Meadows at the northern tip of Newfoundland, so we decided to make that the goal of our journey.

Voyaging in a small wooden sailing vessel is, contrary to uninformed opinion, generally an unpleasant business. Seasickness in the early stages, followed by creeping damp and then miserable saturation are one's lot. The ocean is an hostile environment. Millions of years ago our distant ancestors went to endless pains to get out of it. For us to spend time and money putting ourselves back in again is, to say the least, unnatural. People's reasons for doing so are many and varied. Some are unique to our own period while others have existed unchanged since the first caveman punted across a river on a log.

For the Norseman of the Middle Ages there was only one way to cross the sea and that was by ship. Whether he set forth with Death in his scabbard to sack a Northumbrian abbey or sailed with heavy heart from a crowded homeland and an unacceptable monarchy to begin a new life, he had no alternative to the clinker-built vessels of his day.

For us, in the late twentieth century, things are different. We can travel almost anywhere by aeroplane in safety, and at a speed which makes the journey itself an insignificant interlude. If you consider the capital cost and upkeep of a sailing vessel, then the expense of aviation fades into insignificance. So why not fly to Norway, Iceland, Greenland, and on to Newfoundland?

There are two answers to this question. The first is that to have any real understanding of the concepts and experiences of the original travellers, it is necessary to make the passages under sail. A typical tenth-century Icelander had a better idea of his place in the universe than many a present-day Westerner. He knew the size of the Atlantic Ocean – not in miles, but in days or weeks – and he knew how small he was by comparison. He had personally confronted elemental forces that could snuff him out at a stroke and he understood that, however great his machismo, he continued to exist in an immense cosmos only by courtesy of nature and his own fate.

Stepping on and off aircraft in different continents and sending men to the moon in a matter of days has destroyed our natural perspective of global size and distance. The sea can give it back.

The second answer is the timeless reply of the honest sea traveller. For sailors through the ages it has been enough that the journey is there and that at the far end of it are new lands where people speaking strange tongues will, we hope, admire us for our daring of the ocean. Whenever a sailor stands out for the horizon there is the secret hope that one day he will find his pot of gold. For some, the gold is the type with which he can pay off his overdraft, or court a king's daughter; for others, it is less easily defined. Viking sailors were driven by this hope, just as we are. Other men may sign on for the odd voyage or pay for a passage simply in order to get somewhere but, for sailors from the days of Noah until the sea shall be gathered up, the journey is the thing. And the everlasting optimism that things will get better.

Fire down below

THE dust devils were skittering around the concrete quay in the lee of Brighton harbour wall. I leaned on the sharp-edged parapet and looked down-Channel. There was no sign of a break in the weather. The grey scud was driving steadily on towards the Dover Straits and the wider waters of the North Sea. Force 8. Straight out of the west.

The seas in the entrance looked ugly but less than downright dangerous. Below me *Hirta* lay alongside the wall, stored up and as ready as she would ever be for the six hundred miles to Bergen. The tide served now. It was six o'clock in the evening on 1 May 1983.

Patrick strolled up, rubbing grit from his eyes. We understood each other well. He was keen to get on with it – we both were – but our complement was below strength at this stage and running through the Straits on a black night with a whole gale from dead aft didn't strike me as a smart way to start a voyage like this. There were more ships passing through there than bugs in a doss-house bed, and they came at you from as many directions. In a 50ft sailing boat you always end up giving way to everyone in sight except 40ft sailing boats so there would be no shortage of action.

Doubts about our crew had been filling my mind all day. We had Ros, who would be busy with Hannah unless desperately required. Chris – fit, willing, a useful hand but at this stage sadly lacking in experience of heavy gaff-rigged boats. Gillie – a capable lady, a known quantity at the helm and as a watchkeeper but half a generation on in life from some of us and not big in the tonnage department. She was standing in for John and Mike who couldn't join till Norway. That left Patrick. I looked him up and down. Six feet tall, powerfully built, constitution toughened by a childhood on the Pentland Firth and a commission in the armed forces, with the sort of look in his eye that would make a firing squad lay down their arms and run for cover; a natural sailor. And me: I'm six inches taller than Patrick and maybe 35lb heavier. I wasn't as fit as he was but made up for it by having been out there on boats like *Hirta* on enough nasty nights to have stopped counting.

After heartsearching for another five minutes over the pros and cons of making a beginning, a decision finally materialised. It was probably the worst one of the whole trip.

Plan of Hirta's *rig*

'Oh hell,' I announced resignedly turning towards the boat, 'let's give it a whirl, should we?'

'Got to be right,' replied Patrick confidently, the wind whipping his words away. 'In the end it'll be better for morale to go than to stay another day and if *Hirta* can't take this in her stride, we'll be in poor shape if things ever get serious . . .'

He had voiced my thoughts exactly.

Fortunately the boat was lying with the wind blowing from forward of the beam. This meant that we could hoist the mainsail while still tied up. Ros, Gillie and Hannah finished stowing down below while the rest of us dealt with the mainsail.

Hirta's gaff main is large by yacht standards, but she isn't really a yacht. She was built as a working pilot cutter. Her boom is 30ft long and weighs 600lb and the sail is made of old-fashioned flax canvas. It is treated with a product that purports to arrest decay and which gives the sail a beautiful red-brown colour. It doesn't, unfortunately, make it any lighter in weight. It's a two-man lift bone dry and once it has soaked up its quota of rain and brine it becomes very heavy indeed.

Taking the ties off that lot in the sort of sea the Channel was offering would have resulted in compound rupture at best, so we double-reefed it where we were. Then we hoisted it and tidied away the halyards and topping lifts.

Forward of her single mast *Hirta* sets a staysail which is hanked to the main forestay supporting the rig from the bow, and a jib hoisted from the end of her bowsprit. Depending on her owner's bank balance she should have a selection of three jibs with the chosen one always hoisted ready to go but rolled up around itself in a tight furl using a device called a Wykeham-Martin gear. This simple contraption is made of the finest bronze and dates from the 1930s.

In any sailing manoeuvre, preplanning is the secret of success. The sea always gives you time but you must make full use of it when it's on offer. Once things start happening, developments have a habit of outstripping one's capacity to reassess matters. Our plan was to motor out through the entrance, then sheet home the main as soon as we felt the real wind. Once that was done we would unroll and set the jib to balance the boat, stop the motor and gallop away up-Channel, hoisting the staysail at our leisure.

Things started out smoothly enough. The engine rumbled into life when politely requested, Chris and Pat slipped bow and stern lines without a hiccup and Ros and Gillie took in the slack of the mainsheet as we motored out towards the truth about our working jib. *Hirta* shouldered the first big roller aside powerfully and the main suddenly found the wind. The breakwater slid astern and we were out, heeling heavily and suffering major helm balance problems. Time for the jib. I throttled back just as the foredeck disappeared under a torrent of flying water. Chris, who was standing at the stemhead by the jib furling line, looked back at me balefully.

'OK, Chris,' I bellowed. 'Give it to her now!' And Chris released the line. The furling drum on the end of the bowsprit spun as Patrick began to sheet in the sail from his remote control position by the cockpit, and then my plan turned to rubbish.

Instead of controlling the wildly flogging jib, the sheet just kept on coming in until the clew of the sail, neatly detached from the rest of it, came up short in the deck bullseye. The sail had blown out before we had a chance to control it. It flashed across my mind that the working jib was one of the only two sails in our wardrobe that hadn't been replaced.

'That'll teach you to be mean where it matters, Cunliffe,' rasped my inner man, but things didn't look like ending there. We now had 200sq ft of finest polyester sailcloth kicking like a dying dervish in the gale-force wind. The trailing edge was beating itself to ribbons and the whole crazy monster was shaking the bowsprit and the masthead with a force which was about to result in serious damage.

When a flying jib blows out you can't just let go the halyard to bring it down because the sail is not hanked to a stay. As soon as you take the tension off, it becomes a raving loonie if there is wind around. Anyone who makes a grab for it in even half a gale is committed to a trip to hospital, if it doesn't heave him over the side first.

Patrick took the helm and I was moving up forward to consider this horror show from the front row when Ros's face appeared in the companionway.

'Tom,' she projected her voice calmly above the shocking racket, 'I don't want to bother you at a time like this, but we're on fire down below . . .'

She had to be joking but one look at her expression told me she wasn't.

Chris, Patrick and I froze where we were in sheer disbelief. A hundred yards into the voyage. The rig was disintegrating before our eyes and now there was a definite curl of smoke rolling up beside Ros's flying hair. We looked like figures in a silent movie when the man stops winding the handle. I don't know how long we'd have stayed like that but just then an awkward wave poured green across the deck and washed the fall of the now redundant jib sheet over the side straight into the still-turning propeller. The confident beat of the engine faltered but Patrick showed his mettle by doing the only thing possible to save the day. He opened the throttle wide. For a few heart-boggling seconds the whole boat shuddered even more horribly than she was already doing but the engine finally broke the rope and I pulled inboard the tattered remains of my best jib sheet tail.

The incident could have cost us the ship. As it was it served to jerk us all back into action.

'You do the jib. Gillie and I'll deal with the fire,' snapped Ros and disappeared.

Chris came aft and took the helm, releasing the heavyweights to save the headgear. Somehow we brought the remains of the jib down to the deck though there wasn't a lot left of what, only minutes before, had appeared to be a perfectly serviceable headsail. By now we had gained a useful offing and the waves were easier. Steam was billowing through the main hatch and Hannah's voice could be heard shouting something that sounded suspiciously like 'Take me back to Dry Land, Mummy!'

Child abuse! Yet another crime to heap upon my already overfull plate. Poor little soul. First we sell her the idea of exchanging her nice snug bedroom and her friends for a tiny cabin in an old boat inhabited by a crowd of hairy sailors; then we lay her world over at a steep angle and institute a

25

horrific cacophony of devastating noise. Finally, just to ice the cake, we ignite the whole proceedings and fill it with black smoke. The first day of the voyage wasn't giving her many happy memories.

Down in the heart of the ship Ros had switched into the reassuring mother mode and Gillie was putting the finishing touches to her firefighting success. She emerged from the steam and smoke-filled galley like a pantomime fairy.

'What caused the fire?' I popped the question that had been bothering me deeply. She pointed to where the flue pipe of the recently-installed bogey stove passed too close to a pine bulkhead.

'The stove got over-warm,' she replied simply. 'I suppose the extra draught from all that wind up there blew it up. The flue was red-hot twenty minutes ago. We've shut it down. It's all right now but you'll have to watch it in future.'

There is something tranquil about women in a crisis. The girls hadn't even used the fire extinguishers. They'd done it all with the one issued to Adam in the Garden of Eden — a bucket of water.

'It's a good thing you signed me on to cover for your gungho mates,' Gillie went on, steadying herself on the charred bulkhead.

'Why's that?' I enquired vacantly.

'Because just think of the expense if I'd let off 1.5kg of your dry powder. Men always panic and grab the extinguishers. You might need them next time and you'll not be wanting to buy any more.'

She was about right. The ship was fully stocked and equipped but we hadn't a cent left over. A Scot like Patrick, Gillie certainly wasn't mean but the capacity for prodigality isn't in her.

Ros lurched across to join us and raised her voice above the steady beat of the engine.

'I don't know about you gents on deck but I think the ladies have had enough for today,' she said. 'Why don't we put in to the next port up the coast? We can have a good meal and a sleep and start again tomorrow. It'll be dark soon and the Straits of Dover would be bad enough with a jib bent on. Without a jib . . .' She winked at me significantly. That was the excuse that was needed. I laid off a course for Newhaven and returned to the deck to find that such sophistication was unnecessary. The breakwater with its classic lighthouse was in full view and Chris was already edging the ship across in that general direction in anticipation of the consensus of opinion.

By 8.30pm we were tied up to a fishing boat in Newhaven harbour. On the middle of her deck was a huge plastic wastepaper basket in the form of a teddy bear, presumably the relic of an improbable run ashore. Minutes later Hannah had made friends with his beast and was happily organising a party

(opposite) North Sea oil

26

for her own stuffed menagerie. The grown-ups sprawled in the cockpit while Gillie poured us shots of whisky that would have stunned a team of carriage horses. We all felt several years older.

Seventy-two hours later with the propellor cleared, 450 miles on the log and the Dover Straits far astern, *Hirta* was sailing slowly through a city of North Sea oil rigs. The loom of their working lights reached us before they came up over the horizon and the ones that were burning-off lit up the night like volcanoes. To be sailing amongst all this brash demonstration of man's increasing power over nature in a vessel of *Hirta*'s age was strange. Chris and I whiled away our middle watch considering the implications.

'In one sense, the difference in years is insignificant.' Chris sipped his coffee, his face lit by a suddenly flaring rig. 'These boys have been out here ten or fifteen years. *Hirta*'s seventy-two. In terms of the life of man both have only been around for the blink of an eye.'

'On the other hand though,' he went on as I steered easily through the night, 'the rigs are representatives of the age of the jet airliner and the microprocessor. *Hirta* was working for her bread while the Austro–Hungarian Empire was in full swing and generals still believed that cavalry would win the next war.'

'That's the difference,' I cut in. '*Hirta*'s in harmony with her environment. In those days boats couldn't fight the sea. The best they could do was live with it and use its forces to work their way to their destination. These rigs are so mighty they don't have to give with the punches.'

'Two million years we've been respecting our surroundings,' Chris warmed to the theme. 'Now in three generations a few of us are learning to control some of the elements, or even drive them back.' He paused and threw the dregs of his drink away to leeward. 'And because one or two brilliant people have given us these capabilities, the whole mass of western man gets cocky and thinks he owns the planet.'

Conversation fizzled out with the moonrise and, after bringing abeam a rig that was belching detached balls of fire at the night, I passed Chris the helm and went below for another brew. While waiting for the kettle I listened to the ship around me as she sailed gently into the night. It was quiet down below; no sea noise with the skylights closed, just a slight creaking from the gaff jaws transmitted to the cabin by the mast which passes through the forward end of the saloon.

At that time we had owned *Hirta* for only nine months. When Ros and I had gone looking for a family-sized boat that could take us more or less anywhere, we had considered most of the possibilities that were available and finally settled on one that wasn't.

For a combination of seaworthiness, comfort, reasonable speed, afford-

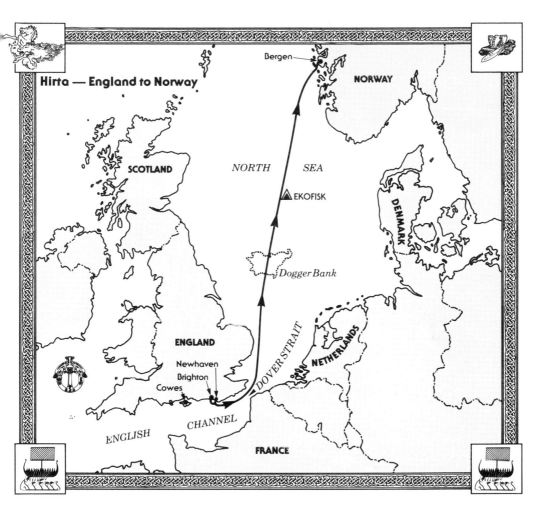

Hirta's route from England to Norway

ability and that indefinable but vital extra, beauty, it had to be a pilot cutter. The trouble was that the last ones were built before World War I and of the few survivors in anything approaching seagoing condition, none were ever likely to come up for sale. But just as the hour often supplies the man, *Hirta* appeared out of the blue at exactly the right time. She had been living discreetly in west Scotland with the same owners for the previous twenty-five years. They parted with her reluctantly but with stoic resignation and we sailed her away to refit her for ocean voyaging.

I poured the last of the fresh milk into Chris's coffee and chased the polar

29

Patrick

bears around with a spoon. He and I had met while sailing a 7-ton fibreglass sloop off the French coast. One evening the two of us were yarning in the cockpit, anchored by the Island of Sark, when he enquired,

'What's so magical about these pilot cutters, then? What makes you buy a boat as ancient as that when you could have something like this instead?'

'The thing about a pilot cutter,' I replied, 'is that they are totally honest boats. They were built without compromise by craftsmen with generations of tradition for the finest seamen of all time. The pilots of the Bristol Channel where *Hirta* comes from all had their own boats and they competed with each other for the best-paying ship.'

'So the fastest boat made the most money?'

'Basically yes, but it wasn't any use being the furthest boat down the shipping lane if the first gale that came along blew you to ribbons. By the turn of the century there wasn't a working boat in Britain could match them for speed, but their seaworthiness in storm conditions had become a legend as well.'

Chris leaned back against the cold stainless-steel pushpit and shaded his eyes from the sun as it set over Guernsey.

'That's all very well,' he went on, 'but that was seventy years ago. You

30

can't tell me there's been no progress in all that time, and besides, boats can't last for ever.'

'There's been plenty of progress but only in certain directions. Today's yachts generally have different requirements from sailing pilot cutters. A pilot cutter would be a lousy bet if you were looking for a boat for a spot of weekend yachting with the wife and kids. It'd be too heavy to handle and far too slow in the light going you'd be wanting to sail in. But for what I need – a long stride, comfort at sea and all that sort of thing – they still haven't been bettered. As far as condition goes, any boat's only as good as its owners have given it the chance to be. If it was well built and has been carefully maintained, a wooden boat can last a hundred years. *Hirta*'s not quite the ship she was when Pilot Morrice launched her in 1911 but she'll do for me.'

Chris was drumming his fingertips quietly on the cockpit coaming. His work-broadened hands told a lot about him that his face left unsaid: there was a dreamy look in his eyes.

'Do you need any crew for this Viking venture?' he had asked carelessly.

Watchkeeping with Chris was always a delight and it seemed no time had passed before the doors to the companionway burst open and our peaceful bubble was invaded by Patrick and Gillie. The Caledonian contingent were not amused by our failure to provide them with refreshment at the change of watch.

'What's this, skipper? Where's the poxy tea?' rapped out Patrick as he clattered into the cockpit wearing a hat that made him look like a KGB agent. Chris's face flashed momentarily across the light streaming out through the doors. He's been around enough to know when it's not the right time to laugh but he was clearly struggling to keep his mouth shut. Personally I was feeling guilty because on *Hirta* we always wake the watch with a hot drink. After being shown the sights and repeating the course Patrick took the helm. Gillie had already gone back to the galley to light the cooker and Chris and I followed her leaving Patrick to enjoy his thirsty watch.

'What's tickling you?' Gillie asked Chris as he gave his round-rimmed spectacles a pre-bunk polish.

'I was just wondering what would have happened if Sigurd Skullsplitter had woken Ragnar Ironfist without a cup of tea at 0400 on the way home from Lindisfarne with a longship full of loot.'

'Lucky for you we don't carry battleaxes or you might have found out,' retorted Gillie and swept off haughtily to the deck. We, who had been found wanting, skulked away to our bunks but as we drifted off to sleep we could hear the watch on deck chuckling in the dark.

It was around this time that mysterious quotes from Edward Lear's *The Jumblies* began appearing in the log book. During a night spent hard on the wind and well heeled over *Hirta* had leaked more than her quota. The cause of this was her black hull. The colour causes the boards to absorb all the heat that's going. They then shrink and the seams open, allowing the water to get onto the wrong side of the planking. This is a chronic situation but a good spell at sea will wet the seams thoroughly so that they take up and become comparatively watertight. The night in question had been the first time the seams had been permanently immersed since the previous summer and *Hirta* showed her appreciation in the usual way. When Ros came up to take the air before cooking breakfast she glanced at the book to check the night's events and found instead:

> Far and few, far and few are the lands where the Jumblies live.
> Their heads are green and their hands are blue.
> And they went to sea in a sieve.

To those brought up in modern yachts with their leakproof plastic hulls the idea of pumping as a regular part of the day's activities comes as rather a shock, but one rapidly grows accustomed to the steady clank of the handle. *Hirta* has three pumps. A smart machine that works off the engine, an up-to-date double-acting hand pump and the original bilge pump, complete with lead piping. Of these three by far the most effective is the old Edwardian village pump which dumps its delights directly onto the sidedeck by the cockpit. Unlike the hand pumps of today, it is so designed that you can pump away for a long stretch without either cramp or exhaustion setting in and this invariably makes it the watchman's choice.

The cryptic scribbler was obviously feeling better about things the following night once the leaking was seen to be getting no worse and after Ros had served up a particularly aristocratic curry followed by a hefty slug of our duty-free booze. The offering next morning read:

> And when the sieve turned round and round,
> And everyone cried, 'You'll all be drowned,'
> They cried aloud, 'Our sieve ain't big
> But we don't care a button, we don't care a fig!
> In a sieve we'll go to sea.'

And there, for a time, the matter rested because the first crack of dawn found us sailing with a following wind into Korsfjord, the southern entrance to the maze of inshore leads which form the passage up to Bergen. We were four-and-a-half days out from Newhaven which, by anybody's standards, is a creditable passage for a sailing vessel. *Hirta*'s average speed was just under 6 knots.

The non-sailor might feel that 7 land miles per hour is powerfully slow going for a boat which was reputedly built for speed, but if he did he would be missing an important point. A vessel with only sail to drive her must take what comes in the way of motive power. If there is no wind she goes nowhere unless she is prepared to use her auxiliary engine, and has enough fuel aboard for this to make any difference. If the wind blows from ahead then she must tack as best she can towards her destination, and even if the wind is fair a boat of *Hirta*'s size would be flat out at $9\frac{1}{2}$ knots. To achieve this speed she would need a capfull of wind, a calm sea (the two do not usually coincide) and some hard driving. This exhausts a crew and is likely to result in rig damage or hull strain, so in practice it is rare for speeds in excess of 7 or 8 knots to be sustained for long.

Unlike a car, however, a boat doesn't stop for fuel, sleep, roadworks or even enemy action of any but the most direct sort. Plugging on at 5 or 6 knots enables distances of oceanic proportions to be run off in a few weeks, but a philosophical approach is required if the crew are to remain contented. What comes along in the way of weather cannot be changed and so it must be accepted, as far as possible without complaint. Each day is taken in its turn and in due course a landfall is reached. On this passage everything went our way after the technicolour start which we were still trying to forget, and we were well pleased with the ship, ourselves and our luck.

We tied up at the fish market right in the centre of Bergen at breakfast time. On the other side of the harbour the masts of a mothballed barque-rigged training vessel towered over the Hanseatic warehouses of the Bryggen. All around us the mountains of western Norway disappeared into the low cloud and there on the dock stood a customs man.

He hopped aboard with his lady apprentice and got straight down to business. Like most Norwegian officials his English was excellent and after a brief session with the ship's papers we attacked the nitty gritty.

The whisky.

Having been well primed about the wretched price of booze in Scandinavian countries we had filled our boots with bonded Scotch to the full extent of the law's permission. Gillie had advised me strongly to plank a few bottles before tying up because she had a ghastly premonition that the authorities would seal it all away or only allow us a derisory amount for sipping as we sailed in their waters. We were all concerned about this matter but particularly she and Patrick who had a nationalistic interest in the outcome. The only crew member who didn't care was Hannah. She was peering through the binoculars searching for a children's playground.

In the event we could have tucked a few bottles away undetected but we were glad we hadn't. Out it all came from our two bonded lockers. Bottle

(*overleaf*) Hirta *in Bergen*

after amber bottle, a litre apiece, every one sealed bar the current life-saver in which only an inch remained. Soon the saloon table had disappeared as all seventy were revealed and lined up like soldiers on the varnished surface.

The officer turned slowly to the girl who was looking hesitant.

'There is something badly wrong here,' he said to me with a frown. My heart sank. A month in Norway coming up, a crew of sailormen, locals to entertain; even Midsummer Night. Surely he wasn't going to impound the nectar. We'd all heard about the Swedes doing it but not our old friends the Norwegians . . .?

But now the gentleman was speaking again, still with his forehead creased but slowly it dawned on me that his frown was one of puzzlement.

'Yo, yo!' he shook his head. 'Where are de glasses, please?'

Patrick, the man of the world, caught his drift straightaway and with the skill of ancient practice he flipped the seal from the nearest bottle and unscrewed the cap. Ros passed out the tumblers, large, from the heap in the glass locker and Patrick poured about four fingers of the best with the air of a demented wine waiter and handed it over with an ingratiating smile.

The officer swirled it round, sniffed and took a gulp. His eyes watered slightly, then his forbidding expression was replaced by a broad grin. He set up six more tumblers, took the bottle from Patrick and poured the shots. Then he raised his glass.

'Velcome, to a fine ship and fine sailormens,' he pronounced solemnly. 'Velcome to Norway.'

The benefits of rape and pillage

THE average norse Aristocrat in the tenth century was a fully paid-up member of the Death or Glory Club. These people arrived in Norway at the very end of the great Germanic wave that swept across northern Europe in the Dark Ages burning, sacking and generally making themselves unpleasant. In religion, philosophy and behaviour they were full-blooded pagans and their whole act was one of Wagnerian excess. Violent death was so common that it was unusual for a man of any spirit to die in his bed, or of anything so uncomplicated as plain old age.

Fishermen, traders, sea hunters and farmers, they were a capable race and early on they developed useful seagoing boats. These were a vital part of the Norwegian economy in the Middle Ages just as coastal transport is to this day. Moving anything by land over the mountains and around the deep sea fingers of the fjords is not a practicable proposition, so the water provides the road.

This topography made conditions for agriculture far from ideal but for a while it brought some unexpected benefits. All Norsemen were prepared to go to astonishing lengths to protect their pride. If you had impugned his honour, you could not expect much in the way of small change from a well-born Norwegian of the eighth century. The only method of averting a nasty physical confrontation was to make an immediate cash payment, and since no-one ever enjoys stumping up for anything the best way for these people to avoid trouble was to stay out of one another's way. Every patch of fertile land down Norway's coastal strip was inhabited by its own crowd of characters. The mountains and the sea helped to maintain

(overleaf) Hardanger: not much arable land here —
one begins to understand why the Vikings were so keen
to leave

37

the peace by keeping each group apart from the neighbours. The first attempts at central government were a long time coming and every chieftain could be king of his own castle.

Norse women were often powerful characters in their own right. It is significant that a married woman did not take her husband's name but kept throughout her life to her own patronymic. If a man named Hauk had a daughter called Hallgerd she was always known as Hallgerd Hauksdottir, just as a son would be so-and-so Hauksson. The only exceptions to this occurred when an individual picked up a nickname. This then became the equivalent of our surname for his or her lifetime and could be used instead of the patronymic. Many women achieved sufficient status to be known by their own nicknames. Two such ladies whose offspring star in this story are Aud the Deep-minded and Thorbjorg Ship-bosom.

A woman maintained a legal grip on her stake in the marital home and if a marriage was dissolved she was entitled to take her share away with her. Divorce was not difficult for either sex to achieve. It was only necessary to name witnesses in public and go through certain formal actions and you were at liberty to pick up the pieces and go home.

The comparative freedom of movement did nothing to lessen the loyalty that many women displayed concerning the honour of their husbands. Sometimes a woman would speak out in the open on her man's behalf but more often she would employ more devious means to defend her family's name. A favourite technique was to needle her husband and sons at the meal table and during the long winter evenings, working them into a lather of self-righteousness against some luckless neighbour to whom she had taken a dislike.

As the numbers of people living in these communities increased, pressure on the small areas of farmland became intolerable. This, together with the fiery character of the incumbents, led to an explosive situation.

A Norseman loved drink, women and luxuries but above all he loved a fight, preferably one he was fairly sure of winning. None of the first three was available in excess in the northlands. He had mead to drink and sometimes ale but no indigenous wine was to be had. There were enough women to go round but these men were lusty fellows living without the moderating influence of the Christian monogamy ethic; one or two extra ladies kept out of the limelight rarely went amiss. Luxuries were in short supply. Silks, spices, precious metals, jewels and the like were seen only in the richest of homes.

Fighting, however, could be had on any street corner if you

looked at someone the wrong way. The problem was that you were battling with your peers who tended to hit back with a mailed fist. If you wanted to be confident of victory without subsequent bloody retribution or intolerable expense, you had to look elsewhere.

All these delights were there for the taking in the lands that lay southward. The British Isles, France and the Low Countries were ideal starting points for virile and fancy-free men from the northlands in search of fun in the summer months. The monasteries of the Celtic Church were often wealthy beyond the dreams of a typical early Norse raider. There was plenty of killing; religious prejudices concerning the natural superiority of Thor and Odin over the creeping threat of Christ were reinforced, and a first-class time could be had by all.

The power vacuum left by the dissolution of the Roman Empire had never been effectively filled and these soft-bellied coasts could do little to help themselves. The scourge of the Norse was born. Word soon got round the fjords and shortly hungry pirates were sweeping down before the cold north wind in fleets of dragon-bowed longships. A new word was coined: *Viking*, which means strictly a Norseman on the hunt for plunder. Before long the monks of the Atlantic coasts of Europe were beginning their devotions with the same prayer every day.

> *A furiori Normanorum, libera nos, Domine.*
> (From the wrath of the Norsemen, deliver us, Oh Lord.)

It was not many years before some of the more enterprising chieftains clubbed together their ships and men. The wild armies which resulted were led often by fearsome berserks worked up into a state of homicidal frenzy and such was their overall fighting potential that cities the size of York and Rouen fell in flames before their onslaught.

The scope of such expeditions for rape, pillage and all the fun of the fair was so enormous that any Norseman who was to be considered worthy of the name had to have served his time with the Viking hordes. And so the economic balance of Europe shifted.

All this mayhem did much to inflame the Vikings' love of winning a fast buck and, since they kept taking the booty home with them, social pressures back at the farm didn't decrease. Things only got worse. There was more to go round now and less need to work for a living, so natural urges came to the forefront and procreation hit a new high. There was also more leisure to annoy one another. For those who weren't about to inherit their father's lands and position, a great deal was to be said for going off on a different type of Viking trip, this time for good.

The locals in Britain, Ireland and the rest had been a pushover for a bloodthirsty Viking but the kingdoms were being bled whiter and whiter. The solution to this difficulty soon presented itself. Why not take land there yourself? There was abundant fertile soil and plenty of slave labour – and so the settlements began.

The new landlords prospered in the fine countries they had grabbed and when later waves of Norse bandits came shrieking wild-eyed out of the sea they met with sterner resistance. Instead of cringeing priests or defenceless Irish peasants they found their own kind; men who would sooner die than be dispossessed and who knew the value of a well-prepared defensive position.

By 870 or so opportunities were thinning out for either the casual raider or the land-seeker, but still the pressure in the homeland was not alleviated. Worse to relate, super-chiefs were starting to call themselves 'King'. This was the last straw. Aggravation with the neighbours with an occasional revenge killing was one thing, but when some upstart began demanding tribute and announcing himself as King Harald Fairhair the stiffest resistance was called for.

Unfortunately for the lesser fry no-one got to be where Harald Fairhair was in 885 without having a large and dedicated band of hit-men backed up by an uncompromising nature. Anyone who argued about paying Harald's arbitrarily imposed taxes was summarily put to the sword, burnt in his house or, for maximum encouragement to the others, blood-eagled. This involved cutting open the victim's chest cavity and spreading out his lungs like the wings of a bird. A few colourful examples scattered strategically did wonders to unify the kingdom.

It was with considerable relief that the news of the discovery of Iceland broke in the beleaguered fjords. Although it was not an obviously promising spot, there was at this period a certain amount of useful land in the island. Furthermore, the climate in those days was such that conditions both for living and voyaging in the Atlantic sub-Arctic were much more tolerable than those of today. By the middle of the tenth century the country was becoming solidly colonised, and a man called Thorvald Asvaldsson, a descendant of Oxen-Thorir, was finding himself in serious trouble in south-west Norway.

The sagas tell us little about Thorvald or his immediate family

(opposite) Dawn in the Hardanger

other than who their ancestors were and the area in which they lived. The writers are also reticent about the identity of his wife but there is no doubt that she bore him a son, Eirik, whose hair and newly-sprouting beard were of such a flaming colour that by the age of fifteen he was already becoming known as Eirik the Red.

Thorvald's place in Norway must have been typical for a minor chieftain: a farm with water frontage, a few cows maybe, and some sheep and goats. Certainly there would be horses, at least one of which was probably a fighting stallion. Horse-duelling was a popular sport with the Viking peoples, particularly as it frequently led to personal violence as a sideshow. Many a grudge was settled for all time as a stallion battle degenerated into a free-for-all.

Whether Thorvald favoured trade or, as seems more likely, raiding, there was undoubtedly a ship lying to a mooring off the beach. Each winter she was hauled ashore and roofed over carefully to protect her for the following year. In addition he would have several smaller craft for fishing and local transport. These four- and six-oared vessels looked like baby sisters of the main family vehicle. They were as sweet-lined as they were practical.

The main dwelling sheltered the whole household and was known as a longhouse or hall. Halls like Thorvald's in Norway were built primarily of timber with a roof of heavy thatch or turf. His could easily have been a hundred feet long. The floor was of pounded earth and in the centre, running along much of its length, was the fire pit which provided warmth and light in winter, and heat for cooking all the year round. Down the long sides of the hall were permanently raised benches and somewhere near the centre stood Thorvald's high seat.

At mealtimes the tables were brought in and the whole household ate communally. Any guest of honour was given a fine chair across the fire from Thorvald and all the other diners would be settled into a strict pecking order which depended upon their rank and current prestige.

Smoke from the fire had to make the best exit it could through one or two holes left in the roof. Additional light was supplied by fat or tallow bowls with wicks dipped in them. Considerable care was taken to render these as safe as possible but they still represented a serious fire hazard.

A man of Thorvald's standing would certainly have had several adult males living under his roof in addition to his own family. These might be old retainers, perhaps one or two freed slaves, friends whose status didn't warrant a hall of their own, and very likely some guests on an extended stay. It was quite usual for travellers, particularly merchants, to be offered a winter's hospitality. These acts of friendship led to one family being able to rely on the firm support of another in times of trouble.

Because of the difficulties Thorvald and his contemporaries experienced in living with their machismo, they found it impossible to ignore any insult, however slight. The blood feud was a part of daily family life and as he and his henchmen sat at their meat in the smoke-filled longhouse, the talk would frequently turn to murder most foul or, as they would see it, acts of heroism and vengeance.

The possibilities for starting something you couldn't finish were endless. Marital problems, then as now, were responsible for many cases of lost pride. Today when a party fails to pay his alimony, we go to court for an order. If a Norse divorcee didn't get her dowry back her father might well show up with his axe and his shield to recover his money in the old-fashioned way.

One typical incident that caused tongues to wag over many an evening fire occurred when a bridegroom demanded that his bride of one winter leave her father's home to accompany him to their new life. After she refused him three times he grabbed her by the hair, drew his sword and cut off her head. The father, whatever he thought of the rights and wrongs of the situation, couldn't let this pass and so yet another blood feud was established between two families.

All sorts of petty annoyances could end in violence and such an affair, once begun, was almost impossible to round off to everyone's satisfaction. 'Like for like' was the rule in theory. Each rank of man had a different money value and a feud could be terminated by the aggressors paying up. This was often arranged and all went peaceably for a while until someone, frequently a woman, decided that the cash settlement was not enough and that her grief could only be drowned in blood. An ambush would then be organised, often at a wellknown road junction, bridge or ford and there, after the exchange of insults with the chosen victim, the score sheet would be re-opened.

Because of the strong loyalties both inside and between families, these skirmishes sometimes escalated into pitched battles with many deaths and plenty of good men maimed. This sort of carry-on was clearly against the interests of the community as a whole and so a rudimentary legal system was established to keep the lid on the can of worms.

(overleaf) A still afternoon near Norheimsund

45

At regular intervals all the important men of a region met at an assembly, known as the *Thing*. Cases of manslaughter were heard and speedy justice meted out. There was rarely any doubt about who had perpetrated the killing. The question to be decided was more usually what was to be done about it. After an undisputed homicide the malefactor would either pay up, challenge the plaintiff to single combat, or submit to outlawry.

Of these unpleasant alternatives, paying-up requires no explanation. When you had a weak case but a strong axe-hand, however, you could insist on your opponent coming along for a get-together known as a *holm-gang*. The substance of this was that both litigants rowed across to a small island or *holm* and slugged out their differences. Since there was only one survivor in a hearing of this kind the legal problem was always solved without fear of appeal.

If you were challenged to *holm-gang* and didn't fancy your chances, the only option was to drop the whole case. Considerable prestige would be dropped at the same time but at least everyone lived to fight another day.

On the face of things the system of outlawry was a sensible one. When a man's excesses of behaviour were such that his continued presence was a constant incitement to the families of his victims, he could be placed outside the law's theoretical protection. Once outlawed it was open season on his life and anyone, particularly those with a grudge against him, could do away with him without fear of legally-sanctioned retribution. Any outlaw with a strong survival instinct, therefore, would leave the district at his earliest convenience.

In the case of a minor crime involving only one or two killings of no great consequence, a man might be outlawed for one or three years. This provided a useful cooling-off period for all concerned. If, however, the nature or number of his atrocities was such that reconciliation seemed an impossible hope, he might be outlawed for life.

Thorvald Asvaldsson, at the time that we become interested in his affairs, was at the peak of his personal prestige. He was involved in a heavy feud with a powerful neighbour, and the atmosphere in his hall was reminiscent of a castle under siege. Several folk must have already been killed on both sides and an action was being brought against him at the next meeting of the *Thing*.

Those of his neighbours who had backed him up were probably installed as permanent house-guests for mutual protection. It is easy to imagine the late-night drinking bouts with negotiations in

48

progress about who was prepared to put up what in the way of blood-money should it become necessary.

The young hot-bloods were doubtless urging a full-scale raid on the halls of their opponents. If they were sudden they might manage to burn them in, which was a favourite method of genocide. But Thorvald, showing signs of growing old, had made up his mind. They would go to the *Thing* and see whether they couldn't outface the opposition.

Young Eirik was certainly well trained in weapon-bearing and he would be listening carefully as the strangely lyrical voices droned on. Nobody asked Eirik's opinion but he was learning fast as his destiny was unfolded through the twilit summer night . . .

THE rain clouds chased away over the snow-covered mountains as *Hirta* sailed south through the sea-leads towards the Hardangerfjord. We were now only four on board. Patrick had taken the ferry back to Britain for a month to harrass his business partners and Chris was away down the Telemark Railway to Sweden. This left Gillie, the girls and me to look after the ship for a short while. It was now mid-May and we were not due to sail for Iceland until after midsummer. This six-week hiatus on the bill of fare was to be used for painting and varnishing and also for absorbing the atmosphere of the Norse homeland. We expected no trouble with the former, but speaking not a word of Norwegian we were concerned about how the latter cause would progress. As it turned out we were wrong on both counts.

Gillie and Ros sat on deck surrounded by onions. The ship's two 56lb (25kg) bags had suffered from deck leaks whilst coming from England, and their contents were making their presence felt. They were up in the open air for inspection now the sun had come out. Hannah was having a wonderful afternoon throwing the 'rotters' over the side.

'Once you've heard Chris play the guitar you'd never think he was a farmer,' mused Gillie as *Hirta* glided through the mirror-calm water. 'He was rabbitting on about sheep-shearing in Sweden all the way from Brighton but somehow it doesn't go with Villa-Lobos.'

'He's not had much luck, I suspect.' Ros pulled a face at a particularly nasty vegetable. 'Apparently he keeps borrowing fortunes to buy flocks of sheep and then they go and catch the sheep pox, or whatever it is they get, and die all around him.'

'Does he have land, then? I can imagine him tramping the fells in the Lake District with his crook and his trusty collie.'

'He says he rents it where he can.' Ros held back her final *coup de grâce* on

Gillie's image of Chris as a romantic refugee from a Hardy novel. 'The last lot pegged out just over the perimeter wire at Gatwick Airport!'

Gillie digested this heresy for a while and then she lobbed a desultory onion at a quietly swimming seagull that had done her no harm. With an outraged squawk it fluttered away, putting as much distance between itself and the semi-liquid offering as it could.

'I can't believe he hates Sweden as much as he says he does,' she went on. 'He must have a girl in every one of those lonely sheep stations.'

'You'd think so,' agreed Ros, passing Hannah a dry one to put back in the sack, 'but Tom says he doesn't.'

It was perfectly true. Chris had trained off to the eastward with his sheep-shears looking like a condemned man. It seemed he was doomed to spend half his working life in Sweden, a country he loathed, because so many Swedish farmers were convinced he had the touch their sheep needed. The money was good and Chris' private farming efforts kept coming unstuck so, as he put it himself, 'It's the Swedes or the bailiffs for me, mate. For a drinking companion, give me an ugly London bailiff any day. Trouble is, they keep taking your stuff away . . . See you in Norheimsund.'

A week later we were there and tied up to the town quay. Norheimsund is a small town half-way up the north shore of the Hardangerfjord and is one of its few decent all-weather harbours.

A casual glance at a chart suggests that west Norway is peppered with perfect landlocked harbours and anchorages. While this may be true in a 5,000-ton ship, there are generally two problems for a lesser vessel. The first is that the water is so deep in the fjords that anchoring is often impossible. The second difficulty stems from the fact that the major fjords are too big to provide shelter if a strong wind should blow up from the other side. You may snug yourself nicely into a port on the north shore then, just as you are congratulating yourself, the wind swings into the south and blows straight in, so off you must go to the opposite side, four miles away. All of which doesn't encourage you to sleep too soundly.

Norheimsund is protected by the mountain wall on the landward side and a small island to seaward. Sailing in past this low island and noting its useful proximity to the ancient town, it was impossible not to wonder how many pairs of Vikings had rowed out there a thousand years ago with their fearsome weapons for a *holm-gang*. However many it was, only half their number rowed ashore again, perhaps minus a foot or an ear, to enjoy the fruits of their successful lawsuit.

I sat in the late evening twilight in the cockpit watching the drizzle drift gently down past the lights on the quay. The town seemed asleep and it felt

(*opposite*) Hirta *leaving Norheimsund*

Islands & Fjords of Southwest Norway

like turning-in time. No Chris today. Then a familiar figure hove in sight, walking steadily up the street, his canvas bag of sheep-shears swinging in one hand. Chris was wearing what looked like the corpse of one of his customers around his shoulders.

'Thank God you're here,' he said with relief as he leaped down on deck. 'Another night in a Scandinavian hostel'd be the end of me. They're so damn straight-laced. I swear I haven't laughed in ten days.'

'How'd you make out?' I asked, handing him my glass of Scotch. He swallowed it down in one then turned towards me with a cheeky grin. The droplets of rain sparkled on his spectacles as he fished inside the sheep jacket and brought out his wallet. It was so tightly stuffed with banknotes that he couldn't close it.

52

Down below Chris showed Ros the money. She leaned back in her seat and smiled beatifically. The ship was back in funds which was just as well because we were almost out of diesel.

Ros had spent the last of our capital back in England in order to provision *Hirta* with enough victuals to take us to the States and beyond. Not having any income other than what we earn there was by this time a severe shortage of *kroners* in the kitty, but all the crew had agreed to pay for their share of the food when they came on board. Thanks to this arrangement the ship was able to remain more or less solvent, and so it was a tremendous relief when Chris counted out his contribution in exotic Baltic notes onto the saloon table.

Somewhere out in the dusk a clock chimed midnight. It was the beginning of Norway's national day in which the whole western population dresses overall in traditional costume and celebrates their independence from Denmark, Nazi Germany, Sweden and everyone else they can think of, including Harald Fairhair. To welcome it in the rain, which apart from the onion day had dogged our wake ever since Bergen, redoubled its efforts and thudded mercilessly down onto the deck.

Gillie opened up the stove and threw on a log. A globule of water fell from the deckhead and landed at the base of the flue with a sudden hiss. The cabin was warm and secure in the soft gold light of the lamps and we sat together enjoying one of those special times when the company is sufficient without the need for conversation. Quite unexpectedly *Hirta* curtsied gently over to starboard, the side next to the dock, and light footfalls sounded across the deck. For a few seconds we waited, looking at one another and wondering who the callers were. They were heavy enough for the boat to feel them but they walked softly, like people well used to a wooden deck.

With a creak the skylight above our heads swung ajar; there was a rattle as something tried to gain access and then, dripping with rainwater, two brown beer bottles slipped slowly down, each in the grip of a hairy calloused hand.

Present-day Vikings and outlawry for Thorvald

THE bottles chinked together in the quiet of the cabin. Through the rain-dashed glass of the skylight it was possible to make out two faces which presumably were attached indirectly to the hands that were waggling the bottles to and fro.

'Do you suppose they're trying to communicate?' asked Ros, superfluously it seemed.

'Old Scandinavian custom,' retorted Chris with resignation. 'They're inviting us to their party.'

'Well I think that's very sweet of them,' purred Gillie. 'We've only been in their town for a few hours and already they're making us part of the community.' She paused and a look of puzzlement spread over her face. 'It is a rather odd time though . . .' she went on but Chris cut in.

'Not for them, it's not. There's only the one catch.' I looked at him enquiringly. 'It's their party but it'll be on your boat. You'd better hide the Scotch. These guys drink like hell on wheels!'

Ros glanced at Gillie, then they both nodded in my direction. Getting to my feet I opened the saloon doors and moved aft towards the companionway with a glance over my shoulder.

'We may as well have a couple of beers with them. We haven't met many locals yet.' But Chris' eyes were glinting as if he knew more than he was letting on.

The companionway doors opened and the rain drove in as I stepped onto the cockpit grating. My slippers soaked up the water like sponges. Outside it was deep grey midnight; not quite dark. On the deck knelt two dim figures, still bending over the skylight.

The nearest turned to face me and stood up. He was as broad as he was tall and had an immense red beard. 'Good grief!' I thought, 'it's the Man himself.' But he wasn't Eirik Thorvaldsson at all.

The giant stretched out his hands in the age-old 'I am unarmed' gesture, totally masking his diminutive companion as he did so. Then he said

54

something that sounded like 'Oi-de-oi-de-oi!' I nodded encouragingly, not knowing quite how to respond but his mate saved the day.

'Oh Kapten, god efening. We are happy to velcom you and, please, you take a dreenk with us?'

'Good to see you,' I responded reassured, although the only item of his anatomy that was visible was his streaming head peering out from behind his colleague. He issued a command and the big fellow climbed back up to the dock and rolled off towards a car.

'You'd better come down out of the rain.'

Nodding politely he concurred and carrying the two bottles of beer he jumped down the steps. On his feet he wore heavy nailed shoes which made his gentle tread a miracle. While he was admiring the furniture aft and also marvelling at how lightly, by their standards, *Hirta* is built, the ship tipped to starboard once again announcing the return of Red-beard.

I felt rather than heard him cross the deck but when he dropped down into the alleyway by the engine he filled the space completely because he had in his hands two large cases of beer. The reason for Chris' misgivings was becoming clear. He had, after all, spent several summers in Sweden with his friends the sheep, so he had considerable experience of the locals who, it appears, are incapable of walking away from a half empty crate of ale or an unfinished spirit bottle. We hoped our callers would be different.

It took three hours to drink the beer. Gillie and Ros sipped one bottle each which meant that the rest of us consumed an average of a dozen per head. This we were later to discover was but modest progress. During our little session our friends Njal (the Small) and Arnolf (the Colossal) learned about pilot cutters and we found out something of the social arrangements of the Norwegian west-coast scene. According to Njal the community divides into the Christians and the Drinkers. Since both groups pursued their own cause with a dedication that is hard for a simple southerner to comprehend, they suffered substantial difficulties in finding a meeting point.

Considering my own rather ambivalent position in this scheme of things I enquired whether it was possible to be a Christian Drinker, or even perhaps a Drinking Christian. After sinking his twelfth beer, Njal's English wasn't up to coping with a question of this complexity and so there, for the time being, the matter rested.

It seemed that our two guests (or were they really our hosts?) were involved in a commune of a dozen or so young men who had put their funds together to purchase and rebuild an ancient vessel of the type known in Norway as a *kuter*. This term means a small ship with a plumb stem and a counter stern rather than referring to a rig type as it does in English. Fortunately *Hirta* is a cutter (or *kuter*) on both counts which saved everyone a great deal of confusion.

It was incredible to us Celts and British the way such a large group could get together without any formal arrangements and operate in peace to one another's satisfaction. We saw it again and again up and down the coast in such diverse projects as rebuilding the old *kuter* for a trip round the world to clearing and flattening land for a new football pitch.

'But don't you ever have any problems?' Ros leaned forward, fascinated. 'When we try to operate like that in England it usually ends with people falling out.'

'Vat is this "falling out"?' Njal was nonplussed. We were about to advise him when Arnolf opened his mouth for the first time in half an hour. Clearly he understood more than he was prepared to admit but was shy of his own spoken English. His mighty face was grinning so hard that his eyes were almost lost as he rumbled something to Njal in Norwegian.

The lightweight looked uncomfortable, then he muttered, 'He says that in our country ve haf a tradition for dealing vith peoples who make trobble. Everyone knows this and so trobble is a rare thing.'

Then Arnolf laid it on the line, nodding sagely as he found his words. 'But ven ve haf it, dere is plenty fon for all mans!'

I looked hard at the way he was pulling the cap off his next beer without bothering to trouble the bottle-opener and made a mental note to give Arnolf a wide berth when he was in the mood for 'fon'.

When we awoke it was still raining. The soft steady thudding on the deckhead had become such a part of life that no-one seemed to notice it any more. So much moisture had swelled the deck planks that all but the chronic leaks took up and the cabins were, for once, virtually bone-dry. Wooden boats all have distinct characters of their own and *Hirta*'s is clearly defined. Fortunately for those living inside her she enjoys a paradox. The worse conditions become outside, the pleasanter grows the atmosphere below her decks.

The stove was well alight and someone was clattering about in the galley making the tea. It sounded as though Norwegian National Day was in full swing in the town. There was a band playing and from somewhere, echoing round the mountains, came the crackle of fireworks, or was it perhaps the rattle of small-arms fire?

Hannah's voice was clearly audible through the open washboard at the aft end of the forehatch. She was deep in conversation with someone on the quayside whose comments we could not hear.

'Oh yes,' she was piping with the deadly candour of a four-year-old, 'my Mummy and my Daddy are still asleep. That is because they were drunk last night.'

Muffled voices filtered through from the dock. It sounded as though Hannah was making herself understood. After the intelligence gathered in the midnight hour we could only hope her audience were Drinkers and not of the other persuasion.

'You can always tell when Daddy's drunk,' she went on, 'because he sings songs about sailors . . .' A terrific thrashing sound reverberating through *Hirta*'s hull told us that the ferryboat was arriving nearby. The 'whump-whump' of her propellor going astern hid the substance of Hannah's next ghastly announcement. We held tight and prayed that it was less socially ruinous than the first. The irony was that we had had our condition of the previous night thrust upon us, but it was too late now to explain our innocence to the dockside loafers, and there would be a good crowd of those if Hannah's past performances were anything to go by.

Ros dressed quickly and, slipping into her blue oilskin jacket, she marched straight past Chris' offered cup of tea and plunged into the conversational vacuum left on deck by Hannah who had turned her back on her listeners to return to the business of feeding the seagulls. We all felt sorry for Hannah, who after all was only telling the truth, because Ros had not yet sucked down her morning tea. In her unrefreshed pre-breakfast state she exhibits social characteristics that would stop Brunhilda and her troupe of Valkyries dead in their tracks.

Ros had been gone from our ken for ten minutes or so when, quite suddenly, the rain gave up. It was as if *Hirta* had stopped breathing. The softly insistent pattering that had been the background to our lives for days was turned off as though the plug had been pulled out of a radio set.

Chris, Gillie and myself found ourselves sitting round the teapot just as before but our lives immediately took on a new dimension. Instead of a vague murmuring and shuffling from ashore made blurred by the constant rain noise we could now hear everything: it was clear straight away that Ros was under siege.

We had come to realise that everyone in the west fjords who has had the benefit of secondary education speaks some English. Many show a great command of the language and some have just a few words, but most are ready to give it a go. Probably the best of all are the old sailors, of whom there are many. They speak the English of the sea – grammatically dubious but full-blooded, clear and confident.

'Yes, the boat is a pilot cutter,' Ros' husky pre-tea voice, followed by indistinct questioning tones from the crowd. 'The mast and boom are original. This is the same rig as she worked with.'

A rising buzz of comment, sounding like a multiple 'oi-de-oi-de-oi'!

'No, my daughter does not go to school. I teach her myself. We work two

(overleaf) Arnolf's kuter *restoration project*

57

hours every day and I think that's worth more than a day spent at school.'

Now we were getting somewhere. She had kicked the local sailors into touch and now was getting down to the basics with the women of the town.

'Yes, I bake my own bread. Wholemeal flour. Dried yeast. Two or three times a week.'

A gruff male voice broke in, slightly slurred in spite of the early hour. 'Oh! English ship! You haf whisky in the bond. Yo?'

'No. No whisky.' Polite. But firm. Shrewd girl! While not subscribing wholesale to the philosophy of Dryden who 'never saw any good that came of telling the truth', Ros knows when to keep the real facts under wraps.

Chris and I sallied forth onto the deck to help out and were met by a remarkable sight. The whole town seemed to be down at the quayside dressed overall in national costume and strolling and gossiping like Spaniards at a Sunday *paseo*. The sea of scarlet, black and white hurt the eyes after the universal grey of the last few days. The men wore short embroidered tunics, kneebreeches and buckled black shoes, the net effect of which had the power to transform a perfectly ordinary-looking office worker into a romantic masculine figure. If the men looked fine, the appearance of the women was a show-stopper. White blouses with leg-of-mutton sleeves were topped by black and scarlet bodices. The young girls wore white lacy aprons tied with red bows over their ankle-length skirts, while the more mature ladies favoured long black embroidered dresses. Both types of costume were set off with heavy jewellery. Intricately ornamented belts of considerable value clasped the waists of all the women, accentuating the fine physiques of those who had them, and doing wonders for those who hadn't. Brooches and massive neck pendants of silver and gold abounded and those who were wearing their hair up secured it with comb-like hairgrips of solid silver that could have come directly from a Viking museum. Like the men, the women wore their outfits with a lack of selfconsciousness that would have left the impression that this was their everyday dress, if you hadn't known otherwise. The long-legged energy with which they moved set the glorious skirts swirling from the hips, and even when they were at rest, the breeze picked up the hems and drifted them out gracefully.

It was a brave picture.

'So, tell me, Captain, what have you for the power plant? I look under your ship; I see no propellor, so it is on the port side, yo?'

I turned and came face to face with a hardbitten old sailor. Beside him, dressed as a perfect miniature of the elderly man was what I took to be his grandson. The boy's white, unmarked fingers were invisible in the seaman's giant fist, which was gentle that morning but, as we were soon to learn, had harpooned whales without number, and had closed on at least one Nazi throat in the dark days of the early 1940s.

60

'You're quite right, sir,' I deferred. 'We have a 60hp Ford diesel. It is arranged to drive a propeller which is offset to port.' He nodded, his buckled shoe tapping insistently on the gritty, rain-soaked quay. He was not yet satisfied.

'Why is it that you have not driven the shaft through the stern post and cut the hole in the rudder for to make room?' he asked. 'Then you have no problems with the manoeuvres. As it is I think you have plenty of fon?' That word again.

I had often asked myself why the people who installed *Hirta*'s first engine in 1931 had not done exactly as this gentleman was suggesting, but had finally reached the conclusion that they had been right.

'It is because the boat is still first and foremost a sailing boat,' I explained. 'To cut into the rudder would be a bad crime and she would not handle so well under sail. It would also weaken the stern post to drill through it. With the propeller out the side like this, she turns beautifully under power in one direction, and the other way she does not turn at all.'

With a man of this calibre as my inquisitor it was unnecessary to add, as was my usual policy when asked this question, that the clever thing was always to ensure that you did not have to ask the boat to turn the way she didn't want to go. He had known before I was born that this was more or less true of all boats.

As the explanation of *Hirta*'s eccentric mechanical arrangements was being completed, a couple of the old man's shipmates came alongside. Soon all three ancient mariners were wandering round the deck handling the gear and passing complimentary or derogatory comments, now mainly in Norwegian. As our party passed Ros she was planning with a handsome middle-aged lady, wearing magnificent cloak brooches, for us all to go up to her home for lunch with her family. After a brief 'How d'you do?' I tailed on after the three seamen and the tiny child who were following the smell of Gillie's coffee into the galley.

The trio were fascinated by *Hirta*'s accommodation. Although spartan by the standards set by modern yachts which seem to be designed with comfort in harbour in mind, she is practical and well thought out. She has no fancy button-backed sofas, hot running water or electronic navigation wonders. Her type of comfort stems from being at home upon the sea. No plush settee can make up for a wicked motion, and *Hirta* is as sweet in a seaway as it is possible for a vessel of her size to be. Her wooden tongue and groove seat backs are at the correct angle for relaxation and her bare solid pine floorboards take no harm from repeated soakings in seawater.

For the three old Norsemen however, she seemed to represent the apex of high living. They sniffed appreciatively at the dark fo'c'sle with its mixture of smells and mass of stored ship's gear. The odours of Stockholm Tar, linseed oil, paint and paraffin mixed up with the general whiff of mildew and old wooden boats obviously took them back a few years. Reaching into a dark recess Gunnar, my friend the ringleader, pulled out a heavy ¾in shackle. He tried the pin and nodded as it turned stickily in his hand.

'What you use for the greasing?' he asked as he inspected the thread curiously.

'That's anhydrous lanolin,' I replied, and showed them a large plastic tub of the precious lubricant. Jon, who appeared to be the oldest, took some between his fingers and sniffed at it.

'Yo, yo,' he said, his English clear but heavily accented. 'This we use on the southern whaling ships. We try to buy now for the fishing boats, but no-one can find it anymore. The sea hates this grease. Where is it you can find it?'

'I'll tell you where he got that.' Chris broke in, peering diabolically around the door, 'but he didn't pay for it. In Britain we have crazy people who go for long swims. Some swim to France and some swim across the Bristol Channel from Somerset to Wales. You know the Bristol Channel in the West of England?'

They nodded, no doubt wondering where this was leading.

'Before these crazies set off they cover themselves with grease. Helps keep the water out, see? But they don't use any old grease, they use lanolin from sheep's wool. It's the best water-repellent in the world. Tom had that tub of it from a lifeboat man in Wales. He was in charge of greasing a crowd of swimmers and he saved half a barrelful. No-one knows what became of the crazies, but the lanolin's still doing a great job.'

The old boys were delighted with this explanation. Like seamen the world over they had an inbuilt resistance to parting with money. We had much in common.

Next they wanted the floorboards up to check out the ballasting, so we duly obliged. They were fascinated to see that virtually the whole of *Hirta*'s bilge is full of iron ballast laid tidily on top of concrete which has been there since she was built, but Gunnar expressed concern that the frames and the inside of the planking had not seen the light of day since he was a boy. What, he wanted to know, was going on under the concrete.

'We wondered about that too,' I told him, 'so I removed two sections with a hammer and chisel. It came out surprisingly easily and underneath all was well. The planks looked old, but then they are, aren't they? The wood was very hard indeed.'

'Good,' he said simply. 'But with the bilge full of iron, where is your water tank?'

'It's right here under the saloon table.' I showed him how the table with its clever extensions is located on top of a riveted iron tank. 'Apparently this tank was taken from an old steam-driven road roller that was being scrapped when the boat was under construction. It's definitely original so the story could well be true.'

Once more their faces lit up, this time at the idea of the old pilot picking up gear on the cheap for his smart new vessel.

While the men yarned in the saloon the ladies had changed into their best clothes and gone off to meet Ros' new friend in the town.

'You lads catch us up at the village hall at one o'clock,' Ros called down as they left, 'and don't forget to put on your ties.'

When Gunnar and his friends had finished their tour and asked some more probing questions, they rescued the little fellow from a jigsaw puzzle that was driving him silly in Hannah's cabin and melted away into the crowd that was still thick although the weather was looking black once more.

After brewing another coffee Chris and I sat in the cockpit surveying the scene and standing by to carry on with the museum-curator act. The clouds that boiled over the mountains were down almost to the snowline. On the opposite side of the fjord the heartless ice of the Folgefonn glacier spilled down in clear view above the towering rock wall that climbed almost vertically out of the lead-grey water. The scene had caught our imaginations and we were discussing the temporal nature of life on earth when held in comparison with elemental things. I was just offering for close examination the bit from the Bible about the glory of man that is as the flower of grass when it became obvious that Chris' concentration had flown off at a tangent. His jaw had dropped and his eyes were locked onto something approaching

A surviving Shetland Bus is dwarfed by a modern freighter

from the direction of *Hirta*'s bow, over my shoulder.

I turned to look and there, walking briskly along the dock, came a woman. It didn't take much to see what had happened to Chris' attention. The rest of the town, the people and the mountains all popped out of focus like features on an overheated lantern slide so that she stood out with the force of an extra dimension. She was wearing a long black embroidered gown over a white lace blouse as she swept down the quay. It was impossible to say what age she was other than that she was in her prime. Her back was as straight as a forest pine and the set of her square shoulders suggested a thrilling inner strength. The gentle lines of her figure were displayed to a discrete perfection by a heavy belt of silver. Her fine dark-blonde hair was plaited and piled up so that the shape of her face was accentuated rather than masked. She had high cheekbones, and a short straight nose, grey-blue eyes that glanced once at the ship as she flowed by, and a subtle mouth set off by a finely-moulded chin with the faintest hint of a central dimple.

We sat there like a couple of schoolboys as she passed. To say that her appearance was striking would have been gross understatement, but the shattering feature of her presence was the way she moved. Pride, grace, dignity and a clear awareness of herself came through from her like a sudden wind, and we found ourselves staring after her as she continued on her way. A ringlet of fine hair curled out of order on the nape of her slender neck, a solitary symbol of human frailty, then the jostling crowd parted to admit her and she disappeared.

Chris opened and shut his mouth but the blood was hammering in my ears and I couldn't seem to hear what he said. The only hope of sanity lay in getting back to the commonplace as quickly as possible.

'I'm going to look for my tie,' I croaked, rising to my feet.

Chris looked as pale as if he'd just witnessed a public hanging.

'I don't know about you,' he began unsteadily, 'but I now realise that I am small, dirty and clumsy. Lend me a tie will you? It might just make the difference to my morale. If I don't do something I'm likely to collapse on the spot.'

We went below and fished out the Number One and Two ties. Number One was a Yachtmaster tie issued to me free of charge some years before at a symposium where I was booked to speak and had arrived tie-less. I had taken a lot of flak for this item of dress from my non-establishment mates but it seemed probable that no-one here would recognise it. The Number Two was and still is the tie of a rear-commodore of the Imperial Japanese Yacht Squadron. It came my way at the end of a rather dubious evening entertainment when a well-known oriental yachtsman and myself exchanged souvenirs in token of our promised eternal comradeship. I haven't seen him since . . . Chris selected the rear-commodore's number, we knotted them around our necks and, with our spines suitably stiffened, shouldered our way through the happy revellers towards our lunch appointment.

It was hard to equate the civilised and delightful family with whom we spent the rest of the afternoon with the desperados who had lived around Hardangerfjord a thousand years before, yet even in the home of those gentle non-drinking folk there were glimpses of the ancient bloodline.

Our host showed considerable interest when he heard that we had been entertaining old Gunnar.

'You want to learn about the Old Days? Then talk to Gunnar. That man is a real Viking. He left home as a boy to go to the whaling and never came back for twenty-five years. There are no seas he has not sailed. In the war he helped run the Shetland Bus . . .'

'The Shetland Bus?' Ros asked. 'What was that all about?'

'On this coast,' he continued, 'we suffered heavy German occupation. We had a useful resistance movement but we were desperate for stores, for arms, for ammunition. So in the winter − when there is no daylight, you understand − men like Gunnar went to the British in the Shetland Islands with small fishing boats, the same size as your ship, and the British gave us what we needed. Then the boats came back, those that were not lost through the storms, or through the Germans.' He almost spat out the last few words.

'Why didn't our navy send you supplies by submarine or torpedo boat?' asked Chris. We were all fascinated by the thought of these tiny wooden vessels with their one-cylinder semi-diesel engines running the blockade of the Nazi war machine in the savage December darkness.

'Because the coast patrols were too tight for anything to hide.' Our host went on, 'There was a very good chance that any vessel approaching the shore would be spotted. That is why it was done mainly in winter and with our own boats. The dark season gives you the best chance of avoiding discovery but if you were stopped, you could keep up the bluff to the end.'

'Were the losses very high?' enquired Gillie the Scot. She had been alive when all this was going on, and the Shetlands are not so far north of the Scottish mainland.

'Many men died,' was the reply. 'If you are sunk in the wintertime, the water will take your life in five minutes even if you are a fit young man.' He paused, musing for a moment. 'But old Gunnar . . . they never caught him. He has cheated the sea all his days.'

In Britain it would be generally true to say that any post-war anti-German feeling has almost died out by the mid-1980s. I wondered about the Norwegians whose experience was so different from ours.

'Is there a lot of hatred still, from the war?'

'Those of us who are old enough to remember what happened are unlikely

(overleaf) Hardanger Fjord in May − Heidi country

to forget,' our host said shortly, 'but we have learned not to show our feelings and, yes, time blunts the pain. For your people though, for the Red Ensign, we have only open hearts, because you make the sea your defence and your fathers kept fighting.'

On the other side of the table Halvard, the son-in-law of the house, silently nodded his approval. A fine, big man of about my own age, Halvard was sipping a glass of water, this being a 'dry' household. He looked the epitome of non-violent modern humanity, yet he and his wife's father had just showed us a flicker of the long memory of the Norsemen of days gone by. Even after forty years it would be hard for a Britisher to do much wrong in this town, but let a German misbehave himself and he'd better look out!

That night, Ros and I sampled the two local dances under the protection of Halvard and Karin, his wife. As we climbed aboard his small car Halvard slipped a bottle into my hands.

'You'd better try some of this,' he said confidentially. 'The first dance is a traditional affair. It may be a bit stiff, you understand?'

Fortified by Halvard's schnapps we whirled through the evening. First the official function where we danced in squares to the unique music of the Hardanger fiddle, then the late-night special where we were treated to the undignified spectacle of the youth of the district bopping in their graceful clothes to the inevitable recorded racket of second-rate English and American pop groups.

The more I looked at Karin the more there seemed something familiar about her. She was tall and willowy and had just had her hair cut extremely short, so the fine lines of her face stood out in sharp relief. Dancing in her scarlet and black with the powerful figure of her husband she seemed the spirit of life, freshness and beauty. What was it about her? But I couldn't place it.

As the four of us strolled back to *Hirta* towards midnight with Halvard and I deep in conversation about our western voyage, I overheard Karin say to Ros, 'It is all right that I invite my sister down to join us on board for coffee? Her husband is away and she has been home tonight.'

'Absolutely,' replied Ros, 'the more, the merrier.'

Karin disappeared into a house doorway and was soon running lightly over the wet cobbles to catch us up.

'Heidi has seen the boat and will come down shortly,' she panted breathlessly.

Hirta's cabin was warm and dry after the insistent light drizzle in the now empty streets. Gillie and Chris were inspecting the level in the whisky bottle when we tumbled in out of the dampness and soon the smell of coffee joined the homely atmosphere of scotch, paraffin lamps and just plain *Hirta*.

Karin looked at me cheekily over the rim of her glass.

'Now I know what it is,' she announced. 'All night, when I dance with you I think to myself "never have I been close to a man who smells like this", but it is the ship that gives you your smell.'

I was still wondering how to take this when Chris came back sharply, 'What about your own sailors. Half your people live from the sea. I bet they smell worse than us!'

'No,' replied Karin sweetly. 'It isn't better or worse; it's different. For us it is the smell of hard work and long winter nights without sleep. Your boat smells of the sea. She smells of the west ocean. She is dark and foreign and it is good.'

It was perfectly true that Norwegian boats had a totally different aroma to *Hirta*, but it would never have occurred to any of us to articulate the contrast in this way. The truth was slowly coming clear. These people were incurable romantics; it was embedded in their genes. Even old Gunnar, the hard-bitten man of the world, had had the ice in his eye when we had talked that morning of voyaging to Iceland, Greenland and the far West. He was sailing again the wide green seas of his youth, full of the magic and the mystery of his progenitors, dead a thousand years and more. The chance remark made by this lovely girl had taught us more about the Norse character than we could have learned in years of book study. Beneath the snows of their cool, well-organised society, a fire is on slow burn.

A sharp knock on the starboard side deck above Halvard's head snapped the company back to the present.

'That will be Heidi,' he said briskly and made as if to rise. But Chris was nearest the companionway so he went to open the doors. Gillie groped about in the locker finding another glass. There was an exchange of voices from aft, then Chris returned. His face was bloodless and his eyes were glazed. He shambled to one side and in stepped Heidi, still wearing her black national dress, still with her head at the eloquent angle she held it when she walked past the boat that morning. She was the lady who had devastated *Hirta*'s male complement with one glance of her sea-grey eyes. And, of course, she bore a marked similarity to Karin, which was what had been bugging me all night.

Halvard made the introductions and Heidi sat down. It was clear that Ros and Gillie were as impressed by her atmosphere as Chris and myself, though without the added ingredient of having their legs turned to jelly.

Then she spoke. Quite what we'd been expecting I don't know, probably something along the lines of a stanza of old Norse poetry, but what she said, and the way she said it, took us all clean aback.

'Ah do declare!' she drawled. 'If this ain't the purtiest l'il boat we've had in the neighbourhood in years. Here's to y'all!' And she raised her glass and took a hearty swig.

Pure South Carolina, or was it Georgia? Close your eyes and you were listening to Scarlett O'Hara. Open them and . . . The twist was too much

69

for Chris. He filled his tumbler with a hand that shook so much that the bottle tinkled against the glass, then he slumped into a corner.

Heidi, it now turned out, had spent many years in the Southern United States with her husband who was a flyer. There she had perfected her Deep South twang and developed a worldly sophistication which had combined with her natural poise to such startling effect. She was enthralled when Halvard showed her the North Atlantic ice chart he and I had been discussing and when it dawned upon her that *Hirta* was going down the old road of the west-Viking her face shone with excitement.

Later, as the short half-night was beginning to show a touch of morning, the talk turned to personal ornaments. Halvard was the town jeweller and he, his father or his grandfather had made many of the pieces the women wore.

'Y'all should look at my combs,' said Heidi reverently. 'Halvard made them for me and they are somethin' else.' She sat forward, her back straight yet supple and her silver gleaming in the lamplight. As she raised her hands to pull the combs out of her hair the company fell silent, awed by the feminine power of the movement. She plucked out both hairgrips together and lifted them away from her head. As she did so, her hair dropped around her shoulders, down her back and tumbled over her bosom, completely altering her appearance as it did so. With that one gesture she had shown the face of her ancestors; women with the power to drive men mad and send them away in their ships to death or fortune; women who would tolerate almost anything except weakness and mediocrity. Thorgunna, the fey Hebridean mistress of Leif Eiriksson, had the power; so did Hallgerd who was individually responsible for the deaths of countless brave men, and finally for the doom of the invincible Gunnar of Hlidarend.

We inspected the combs. They were exquisite pieces of workmanship, but they seemed dull by comparison with the spirit of their owner. Heidi sat there, her presence giving the lie to what Chris and I had been saying that morning about the ephemeral nature of mankind. In a sense old Gunnar had done it as well. There was a magic about some of these folk that was a thousand years old, and which was not diminished by the passage of time. It could have been new this morning.

After Halvard and his ladies had left us with many a backward glance, *Hirta*'s crew fell into a deep sleep. I dreamed of double-decker buses ploughing down the fjords with 'Shetland or bust' on their destination boards. These alternated with images of Heidi with her hair down to her waist pointing sternly to seaward while a giant of a man who looked like Arnolf, but was really Thorvald Asvaldsson, shouldered his axe and strode purposefully down to his waiting ship.

The softness of southern England had become a forgotten memory, and *Hirta* was outward bound across the sea of history.

HOWEVER carefully Thorvald had weighed up his chances of success, he got short shrift when he turned up at the *Thing*. Medieval Norse justice, unlike that served up in theory by more advanced societies, was not interested in who started what. It was more concerned with the status quo at the time of the hearing, and that is probably why the writers of the sagas in which Thorvald features don't bother to tell us who he killed, or why. They simply record that 'because of some manslaughters' he was outlawed from Norway once and for all time.

Assuming that the local *Thing* worked on the customary 'might is right' principle, Thorvald and his supporters must have been dismayed when they arrived to discover the number and prestige of those ready to stand and be counted as members of the opposition party. After a short discussion involving the usual exchange of threats and insults, the protagonists would have named their witnesses and then the agreed arbiters and senior chieftains gave out the fateful decision — fateful not only for Thorvald, but also for thousands of others in generations then unborn and in countries then unheard of.

Once he was declared an outlaw Thorvald knew he had to move quickly. He realised before the verdict was announced that fairweather friends would peel off rapidly if things went badly and that he could well be left to stand alone to face his enemies, perhaps with just a few staunch supporters to cover his retreat.

Back at the home-acre Eirik certainly had everything prepared for a swift departure. The best breeding animals were tethered by the shore and all the family treasures and necessities of life were packed and ready, for there would be no time to lose in the event of a declaration of permanent outlawry. Hoping for the best, Eirik and the others must have hung around trying to look indifferent but listening always for the clatter of hooves as the men rode home with the news of triumph or disaster.

But disaster it was, and the subsequent flurry of activity would have left no-one a moment for regrets as the ship was hurriedly loaded and then rowed or sailed away down the fjord to the sea; she had made the journey many times before, but this time it was different. Now, there was no coming back.

It's impossible not to feel sorry for Thorvald. AD963 was a notably bad year to be outlawed. A century earlier and he could have taken an easy voyage to the British Isles and helped himself to a fat chunk of juicy real estate. Fifty years before, hundreds like him had been making the passage to Iceland and joining the new republic that was showing signs of being a likely spot to carry on the good work. By the time Thorvald received the hard word, however, the general redistribution of the best land around the European Atlantic shores had finished and he must have pondered long and hard about where to go before deciding on Iceland.

Although there were ships plying regularly between Norway and Iceland carrying news as well as goods and people, there was no Land Registry Office in Reykjavik with a branch in Bergen. The truth about how much decent land was still available was blurred by rumour. Not many of the outlaws and refugees who went to settle came back home to report current market trends, so Thorvald with his family and friends at his side could only set sail and hope for the best. His route would have taken him within sight of the Shetland Islands on the far southern horizon and on to the Faeroes where he probably gave everyone a run ashore. The animals particularly would appreciate this kindness and the ship's people would be delighted to be relieved of their incontinent presence for a while.

It is reasonable to assume that Thorvald waited for a good weather forecast from the local pundits before replenishing his supplies, re-embarking the beasts and pressing on to the north-west. If, as seems likely, he was making for the western end of Iceland he probably made his landfall four or five days later either on the great glaciated mountains in the south of the island or, depending on visibility, the Westman Islands on the corner before Reykjaness.

In the early days of land-taking in Iceland it was a favourite gesture on making your landfall to hurl the dais posts of your high seat (objects of great sentimental value) into the sea. The place where they came to land was where Fate dictated you were to settle, though it's easy to imagine a canny Viking who didn't fancy the look of what Fate was offering sailing by to a more promising beach-head.

The best patch Thorvald was able to find was in the far north-west beneath the Drangar glacier at a place they called High-rocks.

Compared with the spread they had enjoyed in the home country this was a miserable spot. The thin soil gave little scope for growing crops, which meant that bread was a luxury and ale in tight supply. Subsistence meat and dairy farming must have kept them going, backed up by the always-precarious business of sea hunting for dolphin, seal and whale.

The social arrangements at Thorvald's new home would be similar to those of the old hall, but living standards were sadly reduced. The house was undoubtedly a wretched affair. Timber for house-cladding was almost unobtainable in Iceland at that time and the walls of the longhouses were built of layers of turf or peat, alternated with courses of stones to provide structural integrity. The roofs were supported by vertical posts set in two rows along the length of the house.

We aren't told about any further troubles in the old man's life. His morale was clearly so low that he couldn't even raise the enthusiasm to upset the neighbours. Eirik, now in his late teens, must have felt the reversal of his family fortunes particularly sorely. In Norway he had been young Eirik the Red, the promising son of Thorvald, a comfortably-off nobleman in line of descent from Oxen—Thorir. He had only to stay alive and pick his quarrels carefully and a golden future was secure.

Now he was just another lad growing up on an obscure farmstead at the bitter end of the far-flung colony of Iceland. He had plenty of ground to make up, but his father was growing weaker; Eirik knew that his time was coming, and he was thinking hard . . .

A femboring, a knarr
and a little cat-burglary

HE time *Hirta* had spent in the Hardangerfjord had done wonders to improve our understanding of the Norse peoples, past and present. On that score we were doing well and no doubt there was more to come, but our stay in Norway was also supposed to enable us to catch up with the normal spring refit jobs on the boat. *Hirta* hadn't seen a paint or varnish brush above decks since the previous year and it was starting to look as if she wasn't likely to in the foreseeable future.

'"A great while ago the world begun, with hey, ho, the wind and the rain,"' sang Chris dolefully as he packed away the brushes and the turpentine. *Hirta* was sailing downwind, as upright as a church. She was approaching Bergen once more, and the fine drizzle that followed us wherever we went had just restarted.

'"But that's all one, our play is done. And the rain it raineth EVERY DAY!" You have to admit that Feste got his weather right, even if he was a conniving old jester.'

'He might have been right about the weather, but you've quoted him all wrong,' said Gillie from the helm. 'What you ought to have sung was "And we'll strive to please you every day". Not that I should care. I want to come north with you all to Flora and to Iceland and to America; and instead I'm going home to my Old Man.'

'Just think how pleased he'll be to see you.' Chris smirked wickedly. 'His socks'll be full of holes, and he won't have had a square meal since you shipped out. A man needs a woman for all sorts of . . .'

Gillie hurled the last of her sandwich at him, *Hirta* gybed all standing and Hannah came rushing up into the cockpit, the sudden change of balance having decanted her 'Paddington Bear' jigsaw onto the cabin sole. I came strolling aft from where I'd been watching nothing in particular from the foredeck.

'Sorry about that, Boss,' Gillie looked embarrassed, 'but I think your man

The femboring

Chris is missing his woolly friends. They probably appreciate a man who thinks a woman's place is . . .'

'What's that, Daddy?' Hannah squeaked, saving me from what looked like developing into a no-hope case for arbitration. She was pointing towards the shore and there, just appearing around the last headland before the city, was a remarkable sight. It was an open boat with a squaresail set, reaching across the wind towards *Hirta* at what seemed to be a tremendous speed.

As the vessel closed with us we began to make out more detail. She was perhaps 44ft (13m) long and her hull was of wooden lapstrake construction, that is with one board overlapping the next. She appeared to be decked over for 10ft or so right aft and both her stem and stern posts were extended upwards above her sheerline in the manner of the classic Viking ship. Her single mast carried the large squaresail and, as we could now see, a smaller square topsail set above it. She was steered by a rudder with a long tiller; from the fact that no-one was standing anywhere near it, we judged that she must have great directional stability. There were half-a-dozen people on board of both sexes and they were clearly more than delighted to see *Hirta*.

As we reached in towards the point at which we would turn to beat the last mile or so to the dock by the fish market, the strange boat wore round so as to accompany us and promptly shot ahead, sailing much faster than *Hirta*. We caught her up though when we began tacking in. Not many nineteenth-century boats could keep up with a pilot cutter on a dead beat, but even so the square-rigger's performance was impressive. It gave us a first-hand insight into what could be done with such a sail on the right sort of boat in competent hands.

We watched her tie up and marked her for an early visit, but first we had to say goodbye to Gillie. Now we were back in Bergen she didn't want to hang around. We were going to miss her and she, whilst looking forward to being reunited with her family, had climbed as far as any of us into the different world that we had come looking for. Climbing off the train we were all riding was not coming easily, but she packed her bags stoically and, refusing assistance, strode off down the wet street without a tear.

She left a hole behind her. Those of us that remained sat quietly drinking tea in the saloon, grateful that John was due to arrive. John, Ros and I were old friends. We'd all met one foul winter's night in the tiny aft accommodation on a 90-ton Baltic trading ketch fourteen years earlier. John was the mate; I was a gash hand, and only a child at that; Ros had entered our lives as the guest of another crew member who had come across her and her chum in the public bar of the *Jolly Sailor*.

'Come back to my yacht,' he'd offered airily. They, conjuring up visions of splendour untold, had fallen for the sucker line. They must have been as green as grass because our shipmate was so broke that he had no proper shoes and had gone to the pub in slippers and pink bedsocks, but for all that he was a charming fellow. In his way . . .

John and I were also on our beam ends and were working our passage to the West Indies with most of the work up front. The ship was down-at-heel to an extent that rendered her seaworthiness doubtful and the owner had run almost clean out of money. As a result of this primary mistake he'd also run out of respectable crew and had shipped instead a band of pirates that the seamen's union wouldn't have looked at.

However, the 'romance' of the situation caught their fancy and the girls came back another day. And that's how it all began.

It was many years now since I'd finally fallen out with our skipper and had worked my way through a European winter back to Ros from the island of Madeira. John had endured to the end and finally stepped off the old ship before she sank in the West Indies. Between then and now he'd sailed many a sea, but for the last few years he'd been chewing on the anchor and teaching woodwork to the sons of the farmers of North Wales. The anchor was catching in his throat, and so he'd signed on with his old shipmate to see about Eirik the Red.

The ferry had been in for a while and there was no sign of John by about five o'clock, so Chris decided to take a stroll round the harbour. I tailed on behind and together we sauntered along the quays doing what sailors do the world over. We admired some of the ships, deprecated others, secretly envied one or two, but never saw one to come near to our own.

When we came alongside the square-rigged boat there was a familiar figure standing on the dock by a pile of bags, deep in conversation with someone on board who we could not see. Tall, strong with no spare weight, and a full blonde beard. It was John all right, but you'd have known him in the dark by his enthusiasm over this particular vessel.

'So this is a *femboring*,' he was bubbling. 'Is she still a working fishing boat, or do you run her for pleasure now?'

'This one is quite new,' came the reply, secretly, from below the quay wall. 'She was built only twenty years ago but her form is exactly as the boats were for two hundred years or more.'

I jogged John in the back and he spun round. After the handshaking was done the man in the boat, who we could now see, spoke once more. He had excellent English and the singsong accent we were coming to expect. He was of middle height, in his late twenties and of solid construction.

'You are the people from the cutter?' he said.

Chris and I nodded.

'Well, please to come down on board my ship. We have to talk, and here we have plenty of beer.'

I shot a glance at Chris. He had an expression like a French aristocrat stepping into the tumbril, but John was already down the ladder, and so we followed.

Right on cue the heavens opened and huge drops of water came sputtering all round us.

'Quick, into the cabin,' ordered the skipper, and ducked through a miniscule sliding door into his den.

The hutch on the mini-Viking ship was warm, damp and smelled of bodies, beer and the tar that is typical of all Norwegian boats. Headroom was 4ft 6in (1½m) at the best. The breadth of the accommodation, which was the beam of the ship at that station, was about 6ft (1.7m) and, of course, it tapered from this to zero at its aft end about 9ft (2.8m) away. It was lit by a swinging hurricane lamp and a small sliding air vent which let in more rain than daylight.

It was hard to discern whether there was any furniture or not under the piles of blankets and simple personal kit that were strewn around but Johann, our host, quickly told us to drape ourselves anywhere we chose.

To say that the four of us filled this lotus-eater's paradise would be about right and we, from *Hirta*, were just starting to absorb the atmosphere when a crash like Armageddon thundered through the ship, followed by another and another. Lots of shouting and giggling came next as the *femboring* tipped crazily this way and that. She was not built like a pilot cutter and she felt every change in weight distribution. John has experienced the return of many a merry crew and he got up, cracking his head as he did so, thinking our audience was over before it had begun.

'No, no!' urged Johann. 'Plenty of room, but please to just move a little so we can get at the beer'. Chris and I shunted along and Johann ripped a rug aside like a conjuror. In the dim light we could see a seemingly endless array of bottles. We were peering at them mesmerised when the door slammed back and the crowd poured in on top of us.

'Do you all sleep in here?' I gasped to Johann as a hefty young Norseman sat on my head.

'Oh, yo!' butted in my tormentor. 'In here, we have plenty fon! Ho, ho!'

John had been carried on the breast of the mob all the way to where the cabin was at its narrowest. Out of the corner of my eye I could see a girl pressing a bottle into his open hand. The chap resting on my head was opening one for Chris and it was fascinating to observe his technique. Like all Norwegian seamen, he used the top still attached to one bottle to lever the cap off the next.

'What happens when you've only one bottle left?' enquired Chris.

'Oh, I never can remember by then,' was the predictable reply.

It was taking a long time to get everyone settled in the tiny space and Chris and I grabbed the opportunity for a quick exchange.

'I really hate this beer, you know,' he whispered across the floor.

'What's wrong with it? It's free, isn't it?'

'It tastes vile, and all it does is make you morose and give you a headache.'

'Nobody's forcing you to drink it.'

'I can't bear the thought of the alternative. Can you imagine being stuck in here for long if you were sober?'

He had a strong point. Just to emphasize it he drank his bottle off in one and someone immediately condemned him to a second. He took it, like Cleopatra accepting the asp, but our conversation was cut off because suddenly I was sitting up and Johann was plying me with questions.

'Are you the cutter that is going to the western ocean?'

Instant fame! How did he know about us?

'I met up with Arnolf from Hardanger at the *Vinmonopole*,' he named the state liquor shop in Bergen, which supplied the hinterland for a frightening distance around. 'He told me about you and where you are going. It is a good thing. Have another beer.'

'But I haven't started this one yet.'

'Never mind. One in each hand is better.' I submitted. There was a natural ease about Johann's manner that seemed curiously at odds with our surroundings. Immediately behind me the heavy Viking who had recently planted his behind on my ear was engaged in a violent struggle to remove his coat while still pouring beer down his throat. I had a fleeting image of Arnolf plunging through the night in his awful car, the snow peaks glimmering all around him, and the beer crates from the *Vinmonopole* rattling in the back as he fulfilled his errand of mercy for Njal and the boys on the *kuter*.

Johann did the bottle-opening trick again and continued with his main subject matter. 'I think you and your friends will have a more comfortable voyage to Vinland than Leif Eirikson did. The *knarr* was a fine way to go to sea – the best they had; but you will be better to windward and you will be warm and dry.'

'What's a *knarr*? I thought your ancestors travelled by longship?'

He studied me pityingly for a moment as the waves of conversation rose and fell in the half-light. My ignorance must have amazed him.

'Loss of life was heavy on the western voyages,' he explained patiently, 'but if they had used longships I think very few would have made it at all. The longship was for war and for raiding, not for the sea journey. She had no freeboard and was not so strong. In the big seas she could break her back,' he made an unambiguous gesture, 'or very often be overcome by the waves. The *knarr* was the ocean ship. All the traders used them. They were fine carriers, and they could stay afloat.'

'How were they constructed?' I asked immediately.

'The same as all our vessels of the period. Clinker-built, but heavier than longships, and much beamier.'

'What sort of timber did they use?'

'Oak for the most part. Thin planks by your standards, fastened together with soft iron rivets.'

That made sense. *Hirta* herself is fastened with iron and it seems to last for ever, unlike steel which rusts rapidly away.

'The planking was attached to the ribs with ties,' Johann continued, 'mostly of withies, but sometimes leather. This meant the ship could move a little if strains became too great.'

'Didn't that make them leak excessively?' I interjected.

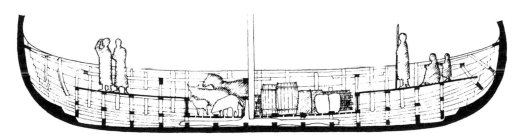

Artist's impression of knarr *based on remains now on view in the Viking Ship Museum, Roskilde, Denmark*

79

He looked at me steadily and took a pull at his beer, as though to punctuate his next remark.

'And your ship does not leak?' he asked simply. I could only shrug and smile. Of course she leaks, and she is of a rigid type of construction. The old Norsemen had a different system, that was all. It had certainly produced results.

A further thud came from the middle of the ship as another beefy soul leapt down from the dock. She tipped once more to meet his arrival and then it was 'all change' as the newcomer jammed his presence into our company. He was welcomed by all hands as the bringer of provisions. His freight consisted of two large haunches of mutton, uncooked but heavily smoked.

A wicked-looking knife with a razor-sharp edge was produced and the legs of meat went the rounds. 'Saw a chunk off and pass the rest on' was the approved etiquette. The mutton was as greasy as an engineer's sweat rag but it helped the beer down most wonderfully. Chris cheered up when he saw it but John was already cutting a slice with the precision of the cabinet-maker. He slipped the dark-red offering into his mouth, hesitated and then smiled a saintly smile.

I turned back to Johann. 'How big were these *knarrs*?' I asked. 'What sort of weight could they carry?'

'They would be 60, 70, 80ft long and maybe 40- to 50-tons displacement. That meant they could carry 20 tons or so of cargo. The arrangements were the same as on this boat, except that the bow was decked in also.'

'You mean that 20 or 30 people at a time, plus animals and goods, would cross the Atlantic in a vessel like that?'

'Yes, exactly. You'll have noticed that all the centre section of this boat is open and has stone for ballast. The *knarr* was just the same. You put in the cargo, you throw out the stone. Nothing simpler, eh? And the animals? Perhaps they erected a tent to keep the worst of the weather off. But the people, they lived mostly in the cuddies at both ends.' He gesticulated with his free arm as best as the crush would allow.

The question-mark must have shown in my face.

'Oh, when you are used to it, you quite get to like it, you know,' he said with a guileless grin. I looked at one or two of the girls and instantly fathomed his reasoning. 'And besides,' he rounded off, 'there is no better way of keeping warm.'

It certainly seemed that my compatriots were not suffering from the cold. Chris had removed his dead-sheep canvas coat which seemed perfectly at home in this environment; in the cosy English atmosphere of *Hirta* it always created a disturbingly pagan impression.

The smoked mutton wandered back from the vicinity where John was last seen. It clanged into the swinging lamp as it came. Johann took the knife and expertly pared me off a succulent slice.

'What did these guys eat on their voyages, Johann?' I wanted to know. I had seen no galley on the *femboring*.

He brandished the mutton before replying. 'Plenty of dried meat and fish. Smoked is better, but more trouble to prepare. Maybe some fruit or berries if they could get it, and *skyr* and cheese.'

'*Skyr?*'

'Oh yes, it is part of the milk when the milk is going sour. I do not know the word. Perhaps something like yoghurt?'

'OK. I've got it. Did they not cook at all then?'

'Not usually. If weather was really good they probably did as our fishermen used to do in these boats and made a hearth with the ballast stones. Then they could light a fire and heat things up.'

'How about sailing performance?'

'It is better to see than to talk. Tomorrow we make a trip for you and you find out for yourselves.'

When all the beer had been drunk we spilled out onto the harbour wall and reeled away to the old Bryggen. John, Chris and I bought ourselves one beer each in a public house with hollow-sounding floorboards and scrubbed wood tables. Like the cabin of the *femboring* it was dimly lit and chock-full of enthusiastic young Norwegians. The only problem was the price of drinks.

Beer at £3 ($4.50) per pint – and the dreaded Norwegian beer at that – didn't go down too well with us. We had a long way to go and, as usual, spare cash was thin in our pockets. In our case, and our case only, the policy of the current regime had worked. We bought no more beer. In the Scandinavian countries taxes on all forms of alcoholic enjoyment are positively penal, the idea being to discourage the drinkers. It discouraged us all right, but the locals have been dealing with this annoying difficulty for years and they have two solutions. Either they rearrange the priorities of their personal budgets in such a way that trips to the *Vinmonopole* or public house become less painful, or they make their own booze.

The one thing the policy fails to do is curtail drinking. It may lower standards of living by diverting funds from other essentials, and it often leads to the production of some fascinating variants on the moonshine theme, but you won't stop a Norseman or woman by bureaucracy – not once they've made up their minds.

Realising we had much to learn, we left Johann and his mates to their fate and went home.

The following morning was bright and breezy. When we arrived at the *femboring* after breakfast Johann and his crew were ready to go. Most of the previous night's revellers had been ditched and the company was down to five.

Johann and a crony at the door to his lair aboard
the femboring

No sooner were we embarked and the introductions made than Hannah gave a squeal of delight and scuttled away after the ship's kitten, a grey-and-white job with all the trimmings, including delicate snowy paws. Carrying livestock is a problem in British vessels because of our quarantine laws and in consequence Hannah, who is a natural-born animal fancier, is normally frustrated in this respect. Any small beastie that wanders innocently within her sphere of influence is instantly mothered to within an ace of its sanity, kittens being a speciality for the treatment.

Ros sighed with relief. The success of Hannah's day was secured, so she could relax and enjoy the company of those young men and their superb ship.

The wind was blowing us onto the wall and so our first job was to row off and gain enough searoom to hoist the sail. Bjorn, Johann's mate, bore us off with an oar and, with Johann at the helm, the rest of us leaned in with a will. The oars were long and heavy but the *femboring* moved surprisingly easily into the wind's eye.

When we had gained as much space as he wanted, Johann laid the boat across the wind and we brought our oars inboard to stow them in racks along the bulwarks. He then handed John the tiller and together he and his four shipmates began to hoist the big yard and its single square sail. Two of the girls we had been squashed in with the night before were still there and they ripped into the musclework quite as readily as the men.

There were ropes all over the place at whose functions we could only guess, but in a remarkably short time the sail was mastheaded and sheeted home and the slippery ship was rocketing away with the wind abeam. John's face was a statement of delight as the boat took off under his steady hand. She heeled much more quickly than we were used to which threw us all off balance, but once she had reached her 'shelf' she seemed to stiffen up and fairly gallop ahead.

As we reached the corner of the bay we turned off the wind and ran before it, experiencing the huge benefits of square rig on this point of sailing.

'Makes you wonder why we bother, doesn't it?' said John.

I thought of the strenuous procedure of rigging a gaff cutter for a dead run and the delights of gybing the whole cumbersome shooting match. I nodded in agreement.

'The crunch comes when we try to beat back,' I said gracelessly. But there was no profit in worrying about that at the moment. The scene was a sailor's delight as we scudded over the calm, clear water down the sea-leads. Hannah was running everywhere playing with the kitten, Ros was engaged in earnest discussion with Bjorn up forward and the rest of us were soaking up the strange appearance of that one great sail and the unaccustomed sound of the racing water as it chuckled against the lands of the oiled oak planking.

'How fast is she capable of travelling, Johann?' Chris wanted to know as we stood in the waist.

'Well, you know, we have no log on board, but I guess maybe 10 knots or more.'

'But that's faster than *Hirta*!'

'Yes, but it's a different type of ship. The *femboring* is light and she is shaped so that she almost skims over the water, rather than ploughing through it.'

'But the *knarr* would have been far heavier?'

'For sure. They worked on the same principle, but being much more massive they would need more wind to make them fly.'

There was no lunchtime on the *femboring*, but after a while the mutton went round followed by a limitless supply of an exceedingly un-Viking variant of the potato – prawn-cocktail-flavoured crisps – washed down with beer. Bjorn was at great pains to assure us that all medieval Norse seafarers would have taken ale in preference to water because it not only provided temporary relief from the austerity of their living conditions, but it was also less likely to give you typhoid fever.

As soon as the mutton was hidden away again, there was a flurry of activity and the boat was brought up as close as she would point to the wind. The beat home had begun.

It was clear at once that the sail set beautifully closehauled and that the only real obstacle to progress was leeway, which was a good 10 degrees. The *femboring* was sailing fast and easily, making between five and six points (55 to 67½ degrees) from the wind. A modern cruising yacht with her tall Bermudan rig will make four points and an older fore-and-aft rigged ship such as *Hirta* may manage a little better than five. The ship in which Columbus and his southern contemporaries staggered across the Atlantic five hundred years after the Norse North American voyages wouldn't make good even 90 degrees after leeway was considered. Compared with our lovely craft, they were crude rattletraps. How did their performance shape up to Thorvald Asvaldson's *knarr*?

'As far as hull shape went,' Johann was saying, 'the *knarr* was probably as good as a *femboring*. Remember always she was much bigger, so she was also deeper. A *knarr* drew 5ft or so and her keel ran all along her length, so she had reasonable resistance to the sideways forces of the sail when it was braced sharp up to the wind.

'The problem they had was with sailcloth. You see how flat our sail is? Good cotton cloth. Tight weave. The best cloth for sails of this shape.'

We had all been admiring its excellent cut.

'The Vikings had only wool cloth. On its own it blew out of shape in no time and wouldn't pull to windward. So they stitched strips of walrus-hide onto it in a criss-cross form. That made the cloth much more stable and the sail set reasonably well, but not like this, of course.'

'I've seen that in ancient pictures,' said John, fascinated. 'I always thought it was just decoration, or artists' licence.'

'Well, now you know,' grinned Johann, 'but even with that reinforcement the sail would not stand as well as they wanted, so they used a long pole called a *beita* to push the luff out firmly when they were sailing on the wind. That did the trick and the ship sailed fine.'

John was gazing at the rig, and it was easy to imagine his mind racing through all the trial-and-error procedures that produced the state-of-the-art tenth-century *knarr*.

'Steering oar, not rudder?' he asked suddenly.

'Certainly,' replied Bjorn, who was now at the helm of the *femboring*. 'It was arranged like a modern balanced rudder so that the ship was light to steer. Also, in shallow water, you could raise it up to clear the ground.'

All too soon Johann, Bjorn and the others dropped us off at the first quay in Bergen and then hoisted sail to go back to their home fjord. For a long time we stood in the late evening sunshine and watched the square of canvas as it drove away before the south wind. John and I were still digesting all the new insights we had gained into the men whose course we were about to follow, but Ros and Chris were planning the passage to the Sognefjord and further north to Flora where we were scheduled to pick up Patrick and Mike, the fourth man, for the crossing to America. Hannah was mourning the loss of the cat.

'We ought to get on our way tomorrow,' Ros was saying. 'All we'll do here is spend money and there's nothing in town life for Hannah.'

We had decided to set sail from Flora because it was a few degrees further north and so could give us even more daylight. It also gave us a chance to explore more of the west coast of Norway but, as we were soon to discover, nature in these parts can dish out conditions that are as vicious as the scenery is grand.

A few days after bidding farewell to the *femboring*, *Hirta* was lying in Leirvig in the Sognefjord recovering from an abhortive attempt to sneak through the leads to Flora. The previous forty-eight hours had been filled with a variety of drama. First, just to see what was there, we had entered a perfect landlocked fjord through a narrow ocean gap labelled on the chart with the name *straumen*. Not speaking Norwegian we hadn't bothered to check what this meant but when we tried to leave under power a short while later the tide was roaring through the gap with such ferocity that *Hirta* could make no headway with the 6½ knots her engine gives her. And so we went back in. We had been lucky enough to arrive by chance at slack water.

John had noticed as we 'ran on the spot' that the place appeared to be black with fish and so once *Hirta* was anchored safely he and Chris had hopped into the red plastic dinghy, taken the fishing lines, and returned soon afterwards with a bumper haul. They had had to wade through the shallows pulling the dinghy behind them, so strong was the tide.

· That evening we left our fjord at slack water and were sailing past the entrance to the Sognefjord when the weather suddenly turned foul on us.

'Never mind,' I said happily. 'Leirvig's well lit. It's not far up the fjord so we'll go in there for the night. There's a dead run in but the dog-leg at the end'll give us some shelter.'

There is also a dog-leg halfway up the channel around some sunken rocks, but there was a lighthouse to keep us clear of that. Or we thought there was.

By midnight we found ourselves totally committed to Leirvig in a full gale and driving mist. No-one likes to enter a strange harbour at night with a powerful wind astern, especially if the harbour has a narrow kinky entrance but, because of the unlit off-lying dangers, in this case it seemed a lesser evil than spending the night in the open fjord. On a clear night in these latitudes at midsummer there is so much light that lighthouses are superfluous, but we noted with interest that the cloud was so low and thick that on this occasion it was virtually pitch dark. As we made our final approach run we hadn't seen a single lit navigation aid. John has X-ray vision, so he was stationed by the helm with the binoculars as I steered.

'Where are they, John? There has to be a white flasher and a red occulting light right ahead.'

Hannah uses a run ashore to experiment with naval architecture

'Sorry Skip. Can't see a dicky-bird.'

'Well we aren't running in any further under sail, that's for sure.' I decided and so we rounded up with a thunder of canvas. Ros took the wheel and steered slowly into the weather under power as the rest of us brought the staysail down at the double and then did battle with the lunatic mainsail. The jib had been rolled up long since. The main was soaking wet, as stiff as a plank and seemed to weigh as much as half-a-dozen large bags of coal, which was probably about right. However, we finally hammered it into submission, tied it up on the boom and returned to the business of looking for those vital lights.

By now the wind was beginning to roar, the driving damp was a living thing creeping in everywhere and as Ros turned *Hirta* round to approach the hole in the cliff where Leirvig was hiding, the boat sailed away at 5 knots under bare poles.

John cleaned the lenses of the binoculars and looked again for the lights. Chris also peered into the gloom as though his life depended on it, which it did. All around were the immense black forms of the mountains. The sea was kicking up and I felt like adding a new requirement for candidates I had lately examined for their Yachtmaster's Certificate, 'Knows the danger of running down onto a rockbound coast at night'.

Ha ha! I thought. 'Physician, heal thyself!'

'Come on, John. They've got to be there. This isn't the Third World you know. The Norwegians don't let their lights out.' This unforgiveable outburst was met with more equanimity than it ever deserved, but John has sat through enough of my tantrums to know that if he ignores me and concentrates on the job, then between us we may save the day.

He handed the glasses to Ros, who also has A1 vision. 'Look low down at the base of the cliff on the starboard bow,' he said gently, 'and tell me what you see.'

A particularly vile gust caught us and *Hirta* accelerated. The engine was still out of gear and I estimated she was making 6 knots now. This was madness.

'It's a lighthouse, but there's no light in it,' came Ros' level voice. God, these two were like icebergs, she and John.

'Check the port bow now,' ordered John without emotion.

She scrambled over to the other side of the cockpit and peered out.

'Yes!' she cried with relief. 'Yes, it's there. I can see the perch. Totally blacked out.'

I took a new grip on the situation, thanking providence for my mates.

'That'll do then,' I rapped. 'We'll take her in, though God knows what we'd 've done if you hadn't seen them.' Chris and John began to prepare the warps and fenders. There now was no ambiguity about where we were as I had studied the chart for long enough to know the way in by heart.

We swept past the lighthouse and turned to port into the first dog-leg, bringing the wind abeam. In gear now, in calmer water, *Hirta* stood powerfully across the wind and took it in her stride. Then came the shadowy form of the perch sitting on its submerged rock. Not a glimmer of a light.

Bearing away now for the protection of the cul-de-sac *Hirta*'s speed fell to 4 knots but that was as slow as she was prepared to go with that wind still blowing. She was safe from the sea, but we had to stop her as she blew past the dock or she'd pile up on the rocks beyond. There was no room to round up.

Fortunately the quay was free and was brightly floodlit. We could see two or three hefty bollards. Ros and Chris prepared a stern line and John got ready to jump with it. I stood by with full astern at the ready, steering as near as I dared to the cruel concrete dock. I was dazzled now by the arc-lights, but John was calling me in.

'Bit closer, Tom . . . A bit closer . . .' Then his tone changed. 'Take her out! Out! Out! . . . In a bit . . . in a bit . . . NOW!' And he was ashore with his rope. He must have jumped a clear five feet, but I wasn't looking. I was slamming *Hirta* hard astern and giving her all she'd got. We could see the rope smoking on the bollard as John surged his turn, then it came bar tight as *Hirta* came to a standstill, her big mooring cleats creaking in protest.

'Bow line, quick,' I called and Chris was on the dock with Ros tending the rope on the foredeck.

And then it was all over – 30 tons of boat stopped from 4 knots in 10ft.

I tottered below and poured John a large whisky. Then I poured an even larger one for myself. Chris and Ros came down looking pale, and Ros peeped into Hannah's cabin.

'You wouldn't believe it,' she said shakily, 'but she's lying there as if she was in bed in an hotel. She hasn't stirred in the last three hours!'

Chris took a swig from the bottle, 'Blessed are those who travel in ignorance,' he announced reverently, 'for they shall not know what hit them.'

In the morning we were still puzzling about what had happened to the lights. The storm had blown through and a bright squally day was shining down the skylight. After a heavy shot of tea Chris and John nipped up on deck to clean the buckets of fish they'd caught the day before in the *straumen*. Down below we listened for the cries of the gulls as the guts started flying but instead all we could hear were shuffling sounds and exclamations of disgust. Then the saloon hatch slid back briskly and Chris' face appeared.

'Guess what?'

'What?'

'You'll never guess!'

'Well come on then, let's have it!'

'You know the week's supply of fish fillets we were going to enjoy? Well, there isn't any left. Only this.' He passed down a classic alley-cat fishbone. Head and tail untouched, with backbone intact but picked as clean as a well-oiled garden rake.

'That's all?'

'That's all, Skip,' said John, glumly stumping back into the saloon. 'It's been a pussies' benefit up there. I thought I heard the patter of tiny feet in the night.' He slumped down in disgust. 'I think we ought to rip yesterday's page out of the log book and start again.'

And so we did – although the log book got a reprieve because when we came to tear out the leaf we found that nobody had written anything in it. Instead of removing a blank sheet we inscribed the date and then entered the 'remarks' column with 'cancelled, owing to lack of interest'.

Then we ruled a thick, red line and set out a second time for Flora . . .

Eirik the Red under seige and Hirta meets the murderer

THE one thing we can be sure of concerning the death at High-rocks of Thorvald Asvaldsson is that he died, so to speak, with his boots off. There were any number of ways a nobleman might go down in action so that his passing would merit a mention in the relevant saga, but no details are given anywhere about Thorvald's death. If he'd been worsted in a fight it would have been incumbent upon Eirik to avenge him. It wasn't in Eirik's character to miss such an opportunity for honourable trouble and the saga writers were in the business of recording colourful events such as revenge killings by people who were, or became prominent, so it seems a safe bet that Thorvald's demise was from natural causes. Because shipwreck was a favourite subject amongst the original saga audiences, the simple announcement, 'There, Thorvald died' effectively rules that out as well. The chance to recount the details of such an event would not have been missed.

Whilst the possibility of a nasty accident with a blunt instrument cannot be completely discounted, the most likely causes of Thorvald's end are illness or old age, or both, aggravated by low morale. He certainly didn't go down in a blaze of glory as once he would have wanted to.

Eirik now seemed set for a life of quiet obscurity on the farm he had inherited at the end of the world, but shortly after taking over the family reins he made the coup that changed his life – and many other people's too.

Although he turned out to be a great man of action, Eirik rarely let his hormones run away with his brains. Somehow he needed to better his lot. Various possibilities were open to him to achieve this: honest labour – unattractive to a natural Viking; trade – not promising because in order to set up shop you needed either goods or capital, and he had little of either; robbery with violence – an appealing challenge, but not realistic in Iceland where the potential victims were all known hard cases; and marriage.

Marriage was Eirik's choice. Later in his life there is evidence of the fact that as well as being handy with shield and battleaxe, Eirik was a smooth talker. At this early stage he must have handled his case with considerable skill because the next thing we hear is that he has married Thjodhild Jorunsdottir, one of the season's prime debutantes. Thjodhild was living with her mother, the redoubtable Thorbjorg Ship-bosom, and her mother's second husband, Thorbjorn of Haukadale, a wealthy land-owner.

The Norse were extremely fussy about social class when it came to marriages and there seems little doubt that Eirik was taking a step up the ladder when he persuaded Thjodhild to set up home with him. A new farm known as Eirikstead in the desirable Haukadale valley came his way as part of the deal and provided him with the leap forward he needed.

We can only guess at how he managed to persuade Thorbjorn that he would be a handy son-in-law. Maybe Thorbjorg Ship-bosom, uncompromising figure though she must have been, was seduced by Eirik's genealogy or perhaps she astutely recognised that here was a young man who was going to go far, although quite how far she cannot possibly have guessed. Thjodhild herself was a stubborn character; she may simply have fallen in love with Eirik and refused to listen to her parents' objections. Whatever the background to their union, Eirik and Thjodhild settled down peacefully on the land that was given them beneath the Vatnshorn. In due course and amid general rejoicing, their first son was born. Like his father, he would grow up to be a man of destiny. The child's name was Leif Eiriksson.

For a short while this pastoral family idyll prospered, but it was not many years before Eirik contrived to fall out with one of his neighbours. Once again, the sagas tantalise the reader by not explaining what the disagreement was all about, but while they are unspecific as to the cause, the result is recounted clearly enough for the dullest student to fill in the gaps.

Some of Eirik's slaves were responsible for contriving a massive landslide which overwhelmed the nearby farm buildings belonging to Valthjof. The debris may well have caused the deaths of several people, including Valthjof himself. Whether it did or not, the victim's kinsmen seemed to have harboured no doubts about who

Iceland — Chris and Mike attempt to start an Eirik the Red style landslide — fortunately without success

was responsible. Without wasting any time in fruitless talk, a gentleman who rejoiced in the name of Eyjolf the Foul picked up the grievance on Valthjof's behalf and undertook the job of murdering the slaves in question. This he did with the usual efficiency at a spot known as Skeidsbrekkur up the dale.

It would have been quite morally acceptable now for Erik to have paid a visit to Eyjolf the Foul and agreed to a cash payment from him in return for the arbitrated value of the slaves. There the matter could have rested with all parties happy with the result. But Eirik was a young man with a family name for sterner stuff. From his earliest childhood he had grown up with the shadow of the blood-feud, tales of blood-feuds and finally with an actual blood-feud of sufficient splendour to lead to his father's banishment from his ancestral homeland. It's not surprising, therefore, to learn that, rather than trying for the money, Eirik decided to have nothing to do with the courts. Instead of visiting Eyjolf in a conciliatory humour, he strapped on his weapons and went looking for him in the mood for trouble.

He wasn't disappointed, and Eyjolf the Foul was soon despatched

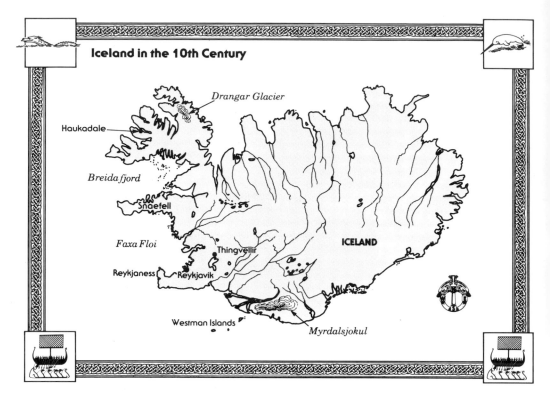

Drangar Glacier

Haukadale

Breidafjord

Snaefell

Faxa Floi

Reykjaness

Reykjavik

Thingvellir

ICELAND

Westman Islands

Myrdalsjokul

Iceland in the tenth century

to join his ancestors at Odin's feast in Valhalla, to which all who died decently in battle were invited.

In order to further his personal security Eirik then sought out another of Valthjof's relatives who had a reputation as a fighting man. This Hrafn had make a speciality of single combat on the *holms*, or battle islands, of the viking world and had done so well in this line of activity that he was known as Holm-gang Hrafn. Eirik pulled the curtain down on Holm-gang Hrafn for good measure, and then went home to Eirikstead.

A man of Eirik's shrewdness cannot have expected to be allowed to carry on as if nothing had happened after an exploit like this. His prestige locally would be riding high following such notable killings, but he had gone way over the top to compensate for the cutting down of a few mere slaves. The matter would not rest where it stood for long. Nor did it.

A selection of powerful enemies brought an action against him at the Thorsness *Thing*, which by this time used to sit at Thingvellir, the site of the *Althing*, the original council of the republic. At the instigation of kinsmen of Eyjolf the Foul, Eirik was banished from Haukadale and, for the second time in his life, he found himself running . . .

IT was a grey and windy morning when *Hirta* set sail from Leirvig to make her second attempt at the passage north to Flora. The night before the harsh mountains that surround the Sognefjord had been cloaked in writhing clouds. Now they were sharp and clear as a flood of dry, cold air came flowing in from a little north of west behind the depression that had made the previous day so interesting.

In no time we had beaten down the fjord and were soon reaching past the *straumen* where John and Chris had caught fish enough for all the cats of Sogne. Ahead of us the first lead into the passages that trend to the north-west behind the islands lay in waiting. On the windward side of the narrow channel the first island was nothing more than a huge mountain peak sticking up out of the sea. Fully 2,000ft (600m) high, it rose sheer on our port hand while to starboard, perhaps 200yd (200m) away, the mainland sat hunched behind a cliff whose height appeared insignificant at 150ft (45m).

It seemed reasonable to assume that the wind which was blowing at Force 6 directly from seaward would flow around the sides of the mountain peak island and follow us up at least the first part of the channel. What it would be doing as we neared the exit was anyone's guess.

As *Hirta* sailed into the passage, sure enough the wind hauled aft, and Chris eased the mainsheet away. Dwarfed by the enormity of her surroundings the boat ran into the gap at 8 knots. For a while all seemed well; then all at once things began to go wrong.

Just as the sun was eclipsed by a lowering crag Ros, who was standing by the cockpit, remarked in a conversational manner. 'What do you suppose all this white water is up ahead?'

John raised an eyebrow. 'You sure there's no rocks, Skip?'

I showed him the chart. The passage was steep-sided and completely clear of obstructions, but the surface of the channel certainly had a very broken appearance a few hundred yards in front of us.

Chris squinted at the disturbances through the binoculars. 'There's something odd about it,' he suggested. 'I wonder if it's a tide rip like the one we found yesterday.'

This was a sensible suggestion and, although the water had a look of extreme rage the like of which I had somehow never quite seen before, I had privately decided that Chris must be right.

93

Thingvellir, home of the Althing *and cradle of Europe's first modern parliament*

Then, without warning, the wind disappeared.

Hirta surged on into the eery stillness under the impetus of her own way and the boom swung inboard as the apparent breeze came round to dead ahead. Some seaman's sixth sense, submerged for generations, was tugging urgently at the edges of my mind. All was not well; in fact, I was filled with such a strong sense of impending doom that I sent Hannah below. We then started to untangle the 150ft of *Hirta*'s mainsheet which was trailing in bights astern, left behind by the idling boom.

While we tackled this annoying task *Hirta* continued to move towards the foaming water. The tide as well as her own momentum was pushing her onwards. After the rushing wind we had enjoyed all morning the silence seemed to exert a pressure of its own but as we approached the area of interest we became aware of an energetic murmuring sound from under the cliff. It was like the noise of a far-off express train on a still night. By this time we had sorted out the mainsheet and we stood like four statues, waiting. The hair on the back of my neck was prickling, so strong was the sensation that something serious was imminent, but not knowing what it was there seemed little point in trying to avoid it. The only way out was back the way we had

94

come which would involve a dead beat into a strong wind and besides, *Hirta* was still moving inexorably ahead.

Suddenly the wind came back. An icy blast of air from the seaward mountain slope laid *Hirta* well over to starboard. Almost immediately it died away but not before it had given her an increase in speed. There was no stopping her now and with the tide right behind her she sailed bravely into the circle of foaming sea.

For a couple of seconds nothing happened, then John started to speak.

'We're as green as grass, Skip,' he muttered. 'Johann told us to expect this. It's a falling wi . . .' But before he could finish his sentence the storm-force wind crashed onto us like a giant's fist.

The sails went crazy. The air was blowing almost vertically downwards off the mountain so they could not set, which was probably a good thing for us all. You can't face a 60-knot breeze in your party dress and *Hirta* was wearing full mainsail and the biggest jib.

No-one needed to be told that the jib had to come in fast. It had already blown out and was shaking the forerigging about in real determination to do serious damage. John and Chris were on their way forward without waiting to be told. They tried to roll the jib up but the weight of wind in it rendered the furling mechanism useless. We couldn't turn the ship to blanket the sail behind the main because the channel was too tight. Then we saw John go for the halyard. It was the only chance we had, but I went cold inside when I thought what would happen when he let it go.

The noise was indescribable as the icy wind howled downwards onto the thundering canvas but, at considerable risk to life, we managed to smother the remains of the jib. Ros started the engine and kept the boat in mid-channel as the rest of us turned our attention to the mainsail. There was no question of reefing it; it was either up or down, so down it had to come. In any normal circumstances before dropping the main it is a sound idea to support the boom in the topping lifts, but on this occasion we dumped the lot on the deck and then jumped on it. It billowed and kicked like a circus tent recently collapsed on a troupe of dancing elephants and we fought it with all we had.

Then abruptly it was over. We three men lay beside the temporarily conquered canvas while Ros steered on calmly down the channel which by this time was beginning to open out into the sound beyond. Now we were back under control once more the peace seemed complete until Ros slipped us a low punch containing the facts of life.

'How fast do you think we're going?' she enquired.

'Oh, I dunno; maybe 6 knots.' I replied breathlessly.

'I just thought I'd ask because the engine's out of gear,' she went on casually. 'We're running under bare poles so it must be blowing a good Force 9 still . . .'

We hadn't even noticed the wind once the sails were put to sleep and it had begun blowing across the water again instead of straight down onto it.

'How d'you suppose the Vikings handled that sort of situation?' pondered Chris as he put on his dead-sheep jacket appreciatively. 'They must have known it was there. I suppose they rowed through.'

As usual it was John who came up with the simple seamanlike answer. 'You don't think that perhaps they just went round the other way?' He smirked archly in my direction and I stumped off below to try a cup of tea.

In her cabin Hannah was busy dressing her best bear.

'Why do you keep making so much noise up there, Daddy?' she asked innocently. 'It would be much nicer if you would learn to sail quietly.' She turned her back on me and buttoned up the creature's favourite romper suit.

I threw an extra teabag in the pot. We were all going to need it.

⌁

It was a Friday night when we arrived in Flora, and having been in Scandinavia for several weeks we should have known better than to stay alongside the town dock. Friday is payday. Saturday is hangover day, and Friday night is the Drinkers' night out.

Patrick had rejoined the ship and we were enjoying a quiet evening in the cockpit with a couple of guests. It was eleven o'clock and the sun had just dipped below the islands which sheltered the town from the north-west.

'This is the life,' sighed the Busker in his Eton accent, stretching his rangy form out on the side deck. He made a Dickensian figure with his long tattered coat and his ruffled dark hair. He'd had a busy day entertaining the shoppers with his flute, but not half so busy as the Lottery Man.

'Too right, mate,' barked the Australian who was travelling the fjords with a trailer that converted into a sort of rolling tombola outfit, 'all we need now is a few Sheilas.' Ros bristled visibly as he finished our last can of English ale. 'Not a bad brew that,' he went on unperturbed; then he dipped in his knapsack and produced a bottle of rum that must have cost a king's ransom at the *Vinmonopole*. 'Been a good day on the wheel of fortune; the only winner was me . . . Here, try some of this, missus!' And he threw Ros a dazzling white smile. She held out her glass and tacitly granted him a few feet more rope.

It was a civilised sort of gathering.

Not a sound disturbed the peace of the harbour and for a while conversation faded away into the quiet of the evening. Chris produced his guitar and was comfortably into some Villa-Lobos when the Lottery Man leaned across to me and spoke softly but with all the wisdom of an old campaigner.

'You'd better hide the whisky, Captain,' he winked confidentially. 'Here comes trouble.'

I looked around but there was no-one in sight, then slowly the presence of a small outboard engine seeped into the corner of my impression of the world. The sound grew and grew until soon everyone could hear it. Superimposed over the buzz of the motor were the over-loud shouts and comments of the occupants trying to make themselves heard above the noise.

'I say,' observed the Busker, 'those chaps must be well lit-up! It sounds as though they're coming this way.'

'Knowing our luck, they'll be headed straight for us.' Chris slapped the face of the guitar resignedly and went below to stow it away. Patrick followed him clutching the litre of Scotch as though it were a new-born baby.

'What about the rum?' asked Ros.

'Ah,' said the Lottery Man knowledgeably. 'When you've dealt with as many of these jokers as I have, you'll know that you always keep what the stockmen call a sacrificial bottle out in the open. You offer them a hit of that and you tell 'em it's all you've got. It doesn't take a minute for them to finish it. Then they push off and you can get back to the serious stuff.'

At that moment a tiny plastic boat, with an enormous cuddy like a garden shed on the front, shot round the corner of the dock. It leaned over crazily as the driver tried to execute an over-tight turn, and an empty bottle was flung into the air to splash down in its wake. The boat appeared to be full of bodies but as it crashed sickeningly into *Hirta*'s port side and contrived to come to a standstill it was clear that it contained only three men. The illusion of multitudes was created by their rapid random motion.

John stoically hung a motor tyre over the side between us and them as they swarmed uninvited over the rail.

'I wonder if they're peaceful,' whispered Ros as a lean young fellow with curly red hair and a straggly beard pressed a bottle of cloudy fluid into Patrick's hands and opened a second for himself. The others came aboard now, similarly equipped. One was an underweight character with nothing to say and a glazed look in his eyes. He was introduced as the Minke. The other gave no name but was notable for a classic, if rather effete, appearance and a hunted expression. He spoke excellent English.

'Looks like we're stuck with these boys,' the Lottery Man nudged me when everyone was settled again. 'They've brought their own. I wouldn't touch it if I were you. It'll probably turn you blind.'

It seemed that Pretty-boy and the Minke worked on the oil-rigs while Redbeard had a job in a butcher's shop somewhere. Round about midnight there was a rumpus on the dock and an enormous man fetched up alongside demanding an immediate audience with someone. Pretty-boy was busy chatting up Rosalind by this time but when he saw the big fellow all the bounce drained out of him and his face took on the colour of a gravestone.

'Oh, you know this man over here?' he stuttered.

97

'No, actually,' replied Ros.

'He is going to kill me,' was the stunning announcement.

'What, here and now?' Ros wanted to know, but terror had robbed the oil-man of speech.

There was a brief hiatus and then the Murderer leapt aboard with a bellow of triumph as he clapped eyes on his quarry. His face was the face of a fighter who has lost enough brawls to have learnt how to win his next one or two and he smelled as though he had stiffened his morale with a strong tot of after-shave. His eyes were wild and most of us were reticent about standing in his way. Ros, however, clearly felt equal to the situation and stepped neatly between him and his victim.

'I'm sorry to bother you at a time like this,' she began, tapping the giant low in the chest with her index finger, 'but I understand you have business with this gentleman.' She indicated the handsome oil-man, who seemed to be recovering some of his spine.

'Yo, plenty business,' was the surprised response. His manner made it plain that he was unused to being interrupted.

'Then I'd be truly grateful if you would conduct your affairs on the quay, not on board my ship,' she stated firmly, and then added rather lamely, 'it's the mess, you know.'

The man grunted deep in his barrel chest and make a gesture indicating that Pretty-boy should get himself up to the dock pronto. There was little alternative but to comply and the two disappeared behind an oversized packing case. We heard a good deal of shouting, followed by a scuffle and the odd solid thump. Neither of the participants reappeared.

'I'll say one thing,' drawled the Lottery Man laconically. 'That'll cut down the drain on the rum bottle by at least one.' And he poured all present a couple of fingers worth, which finished it off neatly.

An hour later the sun rose once more and our uninvited guests wandered off ashore after expressing grave concern at the lack of meat on board. Meat in Norway is the same sort of price as caviar in the Kalahari Desert so, needless to say, *Hirta* didn't have any. All hands were content with fresh fish caught daily by ourselves.

Once the serious Drinkers had left, *Hirta*'s crowd turned in, leaving the Old Etonian and the Australian talking contentedly on the taffrail.

At four o'clock there was a quiet tap on the deck above my berth in the forecabin and the Busker's face appeared at the forehatch.

'What's up?'

'It's the butcher boy. He's just stopped by with a big sack of something. I think Tom had better check it out. His mates are here as well.'

'Oh no,' groaned Ros. 'Not all of them? I thought some were dead!'

'No, there's only the Minke and Pretty-boy. He's all bandaged up, but he's full of himself now. I should stay put if I were you.'

I trudged aft and up into the sunlit cockpit. Redbeard was proudly heaving his sack inboard.

'Is for you,' he announced solemnly. 'Now perhaps we take another drink together and eat one of the sheeps.'

The bag was full of smoked mutton legs of the excellent type of which we had gorged aboard the *femboring*.

'Where is this from?' I asked suspiciously.

'Don't ask, mate,' cut in the Lottery Man, squinting at the early sun. 'Just get it inside and we'll all have a night-cap.'

I pondered on this briefly. If the gift were above board it would be unthinkable to turn it away. If it wasn't and I refused it, Redbeard stood a double chance of being caught in possession of the goods. As usual the Gambler was right, so I passed the sack like a hot brick down to Patrick who was appearing in the companionway fresh from his Arctic-special sleeping bag.

'What the hell's this?' he snapped as the point of one of the short bones caught him perfectly on the bare toe.

'Just whip it into the fo'c'sle and help yourself,' I replied. A minute later he was back, his face wreathed in smiles at the prospect of real meat for the whole voyage.

At six o'clock when the post boat came in, the Minke, who still hadn't broken his silence, suddenly began hitting Pretty-boy over the head with a mutton bone. We didn't known the substance of either of his quarrels but Pretty-boy must have had a remarkable capacity for upsetting people. However, his resistance was clearly weakened by his earlier encounter with the Murderer and he sank to his knees with misty eyes at the third stroke. Patrick and the Busker rolled him over the rail into the little plastic boat with the big garden shed, and his mates took the hint.

The noisy outboard motor started on the second pull and, swaying madly this way and that, the hideous vessel disappeared away up the fjord. We had no idea where our callers were going nor where they had come from, but the next day the legs of mutton were all hanging in the fo'c'sle and we were grateful for their visit.

All that was needed now was Mike Barker, and we were set to say farewell to the Old Continent and go west-Viking, but although we didn't know it we had just one more character to meet who would demonstrate to the full the one aspect of the old Norse personality that so far had been missing from our journey.

The Vikings admired two characteristics above all others. One was courage and a readiness to do violence where one's pride demanded it. The other was cunning. If a person exhibited both features, then he or she would enjoy maximum prestige, but if a man or woman was not physically strong or did not have direct access to powerful friends and relations, then the achievement of a desired result by resource to craft, particularly to a long-term plan, would be equally applauded.

Away in the outer fringe islands on the ocean edge was an isolated community where an elderly lady was quietly and systematically working out her own private system of justice. She was to be our last touch with continental Europe.

Two blood-feuds
a thousand years apart

AS soon as he was banished from Haukadale, Eirik the Red gathered his family and his possessions together and beat a hasty retreat to the shores of the Breidafjord. This vast, west-facing body of water was far enough to the southward to keep him out of trouble with the relatives of his victims.

From the moment of his banishment it was 'open season' on Eirik, and he left Eirikstead in such a hurry that he hadn't time to pack up all his gear. The most important items that he left behind were the intricately carved dais posts of his high seat. These were of considerable monetary value, to say nothing of their mystical importance. It is difficult to understand why Eirik didn't abandon something else rather than these vital pieces; the sagas don't help unravel the mystery. They simply announce that he lent them to a neighbouring landowner named Thorgest. Probably Thorgest came to clear up after Eirik's departure, with the arrangement already made that he would take care of the posts until Eirik was able to return and pick them up.

All that winter Eirik the Red lay low at Breidafjord. The following spring he set up his new homestead on Oxen Island. As he and Thjodhild laid out their furniture there was an eloquent gap around the high seat where the dais posts should have been, and so it was decided that the time had come to go and collect them.

It's a safe bet that Eirik didn't return alone to the Haukadale district. He took some friends and followers along in case of trouble from his old enemies, and the group probably travelled as surreptitiously as possible. Eirik got trouble all right, but not from the direction he was expecting.

When he arrived at Thorgest's place, Breidabolstead, his welcome was less than cordial and Thorgest capped this unpleasantness by

101

refusing to return Eirik's property. Backed by his body of armed men Eirik was able to enforce his claim and he helped himself to what appears to have been rightfully his, without encountering any physical resistance.

As soon as he had left, Thorgest called his sons together and set off in pursuit. He would have had no difficulty in raising a posse because the name of Eirik the Red was at the top of the 'wanted list' in several of the great halls of the region.

Thorgest can't have been much of a general officer because with Eirik and his men in full strategic retreat and he in possession of potentially overwhelming forces, he still managed to lose the ensuing battle which took place near Eirik's old farm at Drangar.

The usual scenario for a show-down in these sort of circumstances was for the aggressors, in this case Thorgest and his boys, to set up an ambush in order to gain an advantage at the outset. Probably on account of numerical superiority Thorgest felt he needn't bother with such sophistication, but he underestimated the first-class fighting men he was up against.

A tenth-century Icelandic skirmish bore no resemblance to the neat, deadly precision of the rapier work of a later age. The nature of Viking weaponry made mêlées of this type extremely messy affairs. Swords were generally heavy, the axe was favoured by many combatants and the long-spiked halberd could produce spectacular results. There is more than one account of a man running his adversary through with a halberd and then literally heaving him over his shoulder in order to release the weapon to inflict irreversible internal damage on a second enemy. Frequently a luckless warrior would have one of his legs or ankles sliced through, after which his efficiency was sufficiently impaired for the other party to make a rapid end of him. Heads flew through the air and survivors were often crippled for life.

When Eirik and his men marched home in triumph they left two of the sons of Thorgest and several of his followers dead in the field. After such a confrontation and such a one-sided outcome there could be no question of a reconciliation. Now it was war.

For a time the farms of Eirik and Thorgest took on the appearance of minor fortifications with plenty of armed men always in residence to deter and, if necessary, deal with unwelcome intruders. Both protagonists spent time enlisting the support of influential characters until soon much of the Haukadale and Breidafjord districts were committed one way or the other. It was a typical case of the escalation brought about by the readiness of men to enter into alliances without fully considering all the possible ramifications of their acts.

Thorgest chose his moment, and by the following spring had forced a lawsuit against Eirik at the *Thing*. So powerful was the collective effect of his support group that Eirik received his second sentence of outlawry. This time it was only a three-year cooling-off period, but he was warned to keep clear of Iceland altogether.

When affairs at the *Thing* looked as black as this there was always the option of breaking up the assembly by starting a serious fight. The fact that Eirik, who would surely have considered doing so, did not raise a finger indicates that, while Thorgest left something to be desired as an ambush organiser, he was hot stuff when it came to drumming up support troops.

Eirik had to go. The question was where?

In Norway, Eirik was probably still *persona non grata* after his father's efforts in the manslaughter line and besides, such a destination would offer scant hope of a profitable voyage. The coasts of Europe were sewn up even tighter than they had been at the time of Eirik's arrival in Iceland as a teenager, so an honest rape-and-pillage Viking spree to the old hunting ground was out. If he wanted to make something of the next three years he was going to have to do something radical, and that is what he did. Anyone else would have sailed to the east or the south-east hoping for the best. Eirik decided to go west!

It would be romantic to think of this red-maned man sailing off with his followers into the unknown in search of fortune. Unfortunately the facts do not bear this out. Everyone in Iceland knew of the existence of a further large land mass across the Denmark Strait. In exceptional conditions the mountains of one could be discerned from those of the other and besides, it was well-known that Gunnbjorn Ulf Dragesson had seen islands in the west after being gale-driven beyond Iceland.

Furthermore, a man called Snaebjorn Hog had gone across the sea to a land in the north-west with various companions looking for relief from the pressures of a blood-feud. His exile was self-imposed but it did him little good. One way and another he and all his shipmates came to bloody ends before the voyage was done. Eirik would have enjoyed such a fireside tale and would have filed away the salient geographical information for future use. Most significant of all was the story that a distant kinsman of Eirik, Ari Marsson, was shipwrecked in a land out to the west where he lived for a time among Irish Anchorites. This was news indeed. If such a place existed it could well have been attached to the land discovered by Gunnbjorn and which was visited in its far northern ports by Snaebjorn and his ill-fated crew. Ari's land must certainly be to the

103

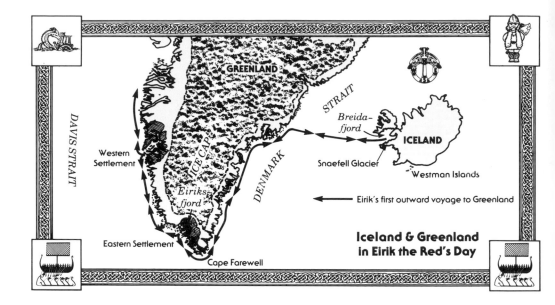

Map labels:
DAVIS STRAIT
GREENLAND
STRAIT
Breida-fjord
ICELAND
Western Settlement
ICE CAP
DENMARK
Snaefell Glacier
Westman Islands
Eiriks-fjord
Eastern Settlement
Cape Farewell
← Eirik's first outward voyage to Greenland

Iceland & Greenland in Eirik the Red's Day

south of the Denmark Strait and if the tale about the Irish was true, then perhaps there would be untapped possibilities for old-fashioned plunder. Even if all this speculation proved groundless, at least Eirik was giving himself a chance of finding a new situation to set up home, in the event of things in Iceland becoming permanently too hot to handle.

Weather conditions in the late tenth century were far more favourable in the high northern latitudes than they are today. There is no mention of any navigators in these waters encountering drift-ice for hundreds of years after Eirik's day. Even so, his was a bold decision, and one that deserved the success which Eirik made of it.

While Eirik and his men were fitting out and provisioning a *knarr* which he presumably had standing by pending the decision at the *Thing*, Thorgest and his supporters were, in the words of the saga, 'scouring the islands' for him. Fortunately Eirik's friends proved staunch and he was well hidden by Eyjolf of Svin Island while the manhunt went on all around him. Tensions must have been unbearable as Eirik's party cautiously got their gear together and waited in a lather of impatience for a fair wind. It would have been pointless to try to beat out of Breidafjord because all the surrounding farmsteaders would see them go and someone would advise the vigilantes. A contest to windward with Death as the prize would have been the only conclusion, so the last thing Eirik wanted was a yacht race. He finally cast off on his own terms and sailed out beyond the islands with his comrades Thorbjorn Vifilsson, Eyjolf, and Styr Thorgrimsson streaming along in company. As the fjord opened its arms to let them go, the other three turned back to the sound of Eirik's raised voice pledging eternal friendship and promising to return to them one day.

As for Eirik himself, he steered his *knarr* steadfastly to the westward as many a desperate man has done since. Placing the mass of Snaefell Glacier astern, he sailed out to grasp his fate with both hands.

On making his landfall Eirik turned southwards and coasted down the inhospitable shore of what we would now call East Greenland. We are told that he was looking for 'habitable' land but we are left in the dark about his motives. Did he want to find a place to live, or was he looking for land that was already settled and could therefore be plundered? Either way he would have been onto a winner, but in the event he had to go all the way to Cape Farewell and begin sailing north once more before he found anything worth considering. In those days the fjords of extreme south-west Greenland would have offered a most acceptable summer vista to a Norseman in search of useful land. There were good pastures, clear streams which teemed with salmon running down from the inland icecap, and enough scrubby trees to fire the cooking for several years. And there was not a soul there.

By the time these discoveries were digested winter was coming on and it is significant that the Vikings decided to make their camp on an offlying island. They would have been far more comfortable up a sheltered fjord, so they must have done this for strategic reasons. Presumably they were nervous about the possibility of being attacked, which must mean that they were still hoping to find men in the area. The ship was drawn ashore and roofed over; then a sod house would have been built and wood and stores organised before the men patiently settled in for the bitter winter nights. At a latitude of 60° north these were much shorter than in the high Icelandic latitudes, but any wind with north in it would bring cruel cold down from the surrounding icecap.

That winter Eirik planned his next move and as springtime

(*overleaf*) *The sun rises just as it did a thousand years ago, but every dawn is different*

105

melted the ice from the fjords he made clear his intentions by sailing up his favourite inlet which he named Eiriksfjord and staking his claim. At that time this was done by the simple expedient of marching around the acres you fancied carrying a burning brand, and announcing to anyone within earshot that the ground was now yours. If there was no-one around to dispute your 'land taking', so much the better for you.

Once he had established the site of his future home, Eirik and his men sailed away up the coast. They spent the remainder of their exile profitably in exploration of the immense tract of land they had found. They discovered a second region of habitable fjords to the north-west of the area around Eiriksfjord and they would certainly have made full use of the remarkable sea hunting opportunities offered in the Davis Strait, particularly if, as seems probable, they crossed over to the Baffin Island side.

The excellent profits to be had from bearskins and sea ivory would have gone a long way towards making up for their disappointment over the question of plunder, for in all their travels they didn't meet a living soul. Narwhal tusks fetched astronomical prices in Europe in Viking times; they were often sold to the gullible rich as unicorn horns, the aphrodisiacal qualities of which were said to be highly satisfactory. Such a cargo alone would have justified the expedition, but by this time Eirik must have made up his mind that back in Eiriksfjord he could found a new colony of which he would be the undisputed leader. By adopting this course of action he would find the prestige and social position craved by all Vikings and his troubles would be brought to an end.

So when his three-year odyssey was completed, Eirik sailed back into Breidafjord to the bosom of his family and the warmth of his friends with his plans well laid. Not everyone, however, was pleased to see him return . . .

THE afternoon after the visit of the Minke, the Murderer and the Butcher, Mike arrived on the fast boat from Bergen and *Hirta*'s crew was complete. By the following teatime we were as ready to take on the North Atlantic as we would ever be.

Ros had made a final round of the provision shops; John had scoured the town unsuccessfully for a replacement electrical component; Chris, Mike and Patrick had checked over the rigging with a care that did them credit and I had tried to caulk an uncaulkable topside seam in the area of the galley. There were no more reasons to stay.

The Busker wandered along the dock with his flute in his pocket and handed us a farewell gift of cod tongues that someone had given him instead of cash. He hated fish.

At the word he let go all the lines except the after spring. *Hirta* leaned her stern against this and slowly her bowsprit swung away from the quay and out into the fjord. When it was pointing the way we wanted to go the power came off, the Busker lifted the loop of the spring from the bollard and *Hirta* slipped quietly away to the westward.

The weather had been unsettled for some days and at seven o'clock Norwegian time Patrick came up on deck with his transcript of the BBC shipping forecast.

'Not too good, I'm afraid, folks,' he announced. 'There's a deep low passing to the north of us and westerly gales in sea area Viking.'

By this time we were approaching the outer islands and already it was blowing very hard. Nobody was disappointed with the decision to put into a diminutive fishing harbour for the night and wait for an improvement. There is no future at all in beginning an ocean passage by beating into a whole gale, but at least we had made a start and we all felt better for it.

The buffeting wind was holding *Hirta* away from the only approachable dock as I tried to bring her alongside. John and Chris stood by to leap the gap with bow and stern lines but when the boat was as near as she was going to get Chris turned and blew me a raspberry and John stepped back off the rail shaking his head. Just then, a little old lady appeared from out of a warehouse at the back of the quay. She looked for all the world like somebody's grandmother dressed to go to the Womens' Institute.

Whatever she looked like she saw our predicament and acted in a prompt and seamanlike manner.

'Throw me the line,' she spoke in a strong, clear voice. 'No, not that one,' she quite correctly admonished Chris who was whirling the stern rope like a cowboy in the Wild West Show; 'the bow line first!'

John needed no prompting and our saviour neatly slipped the loop over the correct bollard.

'Now the stern line, Buffalo Bill!' The old lady hooted with laughter as Chris repeated his performance, but a few seconds later we had two lines securely ashore and could work *Hirta* alongside by using her engine.

Once we were nearly tied up, I invited the lady aboard for a cup of tea.

'Thank you, but not at the moment,' she replied in immaculate English. 'You will be busy with your meal, but I invite you all to my house afterwards for a small drink and a bite of supper.'

'But it will be eleven o'clock, or even later,' interjected Ros, who was thinking about her own grandmother and the rigid hours kept by that honest woman.

'That is perfectly all right, my dear,' replied the lady. 'I am old, you see. I never go to sleep before two in the summer. I shall expect you later.' After giving Ros directions to her cottage she disappeared back into the warehouse which seemed to be the only way off the dock.

The sun was hanging about just below the horizon and the gale had increased in ferocity as we battled our way along the windward side of the island at midnight to keep our appointment.

'This is lunacy,' gasped Chris. 'You can't go visiting old ladies you don't even know at midnight.'

Patrick was carrying Hannah while Ros led the way.

'It should be just round that big boulder up ahead,' she raised her voice above the howl of the storm, and sure enough as we clambered around the side of an enormous rock there was a teeny cottage with all its lights blazing and seemingly hanging on to the cliff-edge by its fingernails. This wasn't the sheltered fjord country. This was the real thing. We were only three hundred miles from the Arctic Circle and just out there the whole Atlantic was hurling itself at this scraggy island. The air was misty with driving seaspray and everywhere was the heavy thunder of the ocean.

John banged on the door, hoping we had come to the right place. He needn't have worried. We were ushered into a warm, lamplit parlour not much bigger than *Hirta*'s main saloon where a table was laid with a snowy cloth covered with dishes and plates of food. Personally I didn't think I could eat another thing – I was full of spaghetti – but we laid in as best we were able and the talk began.

'Yes,' said the lady in answer to a question from Mike. 'I was born in this house. There are three rooms as you see, and we were seven children. My father was a fisherman with a small boat. He was a poor man; he worked hard and we were happy but when I was ten years old there was trouble.'

In between cakes, cups of tea for the ladies and sterner stuff for the men she told us of how some of the wealthier families in the area had been greedy and had tried to squeeze out the less well-to-do boatmen. The consequence was that it became necessary to take greater and greater risks and, in the end, her father was drowned leaving his widow to support the family as best she could.

'Somehow my mother managed,' she continued, 'but we all had to leave school early and work as soon as we could. Me, I went into service and soon I travelled away to England where I became a lady's maid. While I was in London I learned English and I swore to myself that somehow I would see the score settled on those who caused my father's death. For this I would need money, and I was not getting rich in London. Then came the war . . .'

A terrific gust of wind shook the wooden house as this remarkable woman

110

Mike steers Hirta *out from Norway – bound to the westward*

recounted how she had left London at the height of the Blitz and had contrived to find a berth on a convoy ship bound for the United States. Although she saw several other vessels torpedoed, her transport successfully ran the gauntlet of the U-boats and arrived unscathed.

Once installed in the USA the handsome, headstrong Norwegian girl knew exactly where she was going. After several carefully-planned moves she finally was accepted into the household staff of one of the great 'robber barons' of Newport, Rhode Island.

Pay was excellent, but better by far than that she persuaded her boss to teach her how to play the stock market. Before many years had passed the servant girl was stacking money away. She continued doing this for a working lifetime; then, after fifty years, she returned to the island where she was born. She was by then a wealthy woman.

The first thing she did was to buy back the family house, in which we now sat. She was the only survivor of the fisherman's children, but she had nephews and nieces still in the town. They, she said, were not particularly interested in her, but she looked after them as well as she was able.

'But what about the people who put the squeeze on your father? They must be all dead, now,' queried Ros.

'They are gone, yes,' was the reply, 'but their children are my age and their grandchildren still do not get on so well with my nephews. But, you see, I have bought every dock in the area except for one, and that is the dock my father built. They can only land their catch at that dock now, and I am making negotiations to buy that one also, because by rights it should be mine anyway.

'In two weeks I hope to own my father's quay; and then my work will be complete. My family are prospering. The others,' she chuckled, 'the others have a lot of problems . . .'

Suddenly her face softened and once more she might have been anybody's granny.

'But, my dear,' she slapped Ros delightedly on the wrist, 'I had such fun in the States; let me tell you about it all . . .' The two women stepped out into the miniscule kitchen where crockery began to clatter and shrieks of laughter drowned the sound of the storm.

The rest of us sat in stunned silence. Chris reached for the Aquavit bottle and poured himself a stiff shot.

'Christ,' he blasphemed, taking a heavy slug, 'I'm glad we're not on the wrong side of her. She's straight out of a saga!'

And she might well have been.

The next morning the gale had blown itself out leaving a lumpy swell from the west and a brisk northerly breeze. The owner of the town herself came down to let go our lines. Before we left she handed us a small gift. It was an old glass fishing float.

'This is the last of my father's floats,' she said, 'you should hang it in your ship. I think it will give you good fortune.' And with that she threw off the lines.

I gave *Hirta* some searoom and then we hoisted sail and killed the engine. As we eased the sheets the boat heeled firmly. Our friend was gazing after us, her voice carrying thinly over the sparkling sea.

'Good wind!' she was calling. 'Fair winds to the west-Viking!'

And that was the last word we heard from the Old World for many a day.

Medieval navigation in the Western Ocean

ONCE *Hirta* had moved out from the shelter of the last of the Norwegian islands we were immediately aware of what was to become a feature of the beginning of each leg of our voyage. There was an evil sea running, just as there must always have been for every traveller departing on any section of a westbound North Atlantic voyage in a small sailing vessel.

In these latitudes the weather pattern in practice seems to vary from the preponderance of easterly winds we had looked for at the planning stage of the journey. What is often served up in reality is heavy westerly gales followed by periods of changeable weather which endure for varying lengths of time before displaced by the next gale. The effect of this is that the unhappy mariner lurks in an anchorage somewhere, just as we had done, until the gale blows itself out. He then sallies forth with high hopes and runs smack into a monster head-sea left over from yesterday's meteorological excesses and aggravated by the recently veered wind. This tests the strength of his constitution in general and his stomach in particular.

We were lucky. In spite of the extreme motion only John (of all people) and Hannah succumbed to what Mike described as the 'big spit', and neither of them made a song and dance of their discomfort.

The pumping began in earnest once again as we set course towards Iceland and the mysterious log entries from *The Jumblies* reappeared.

> The water it soon came in, it did,
> The water it soon came in,
> So to keep them dry, they wrapped their feet
> In a pinky paper all folded neat,
> And they fastened it down with a pin.

*(overleaf) A beautiful landfall cloud sits on Batalden,
outside Flora*

On discovering yet another facetious entry into the ship's official record, I instituted a surreptitious bedding survey and, sure enough, Hannah discovered that the lower end of Chris' sleeping bag was neatly encased in a red plastic laundry bag secured with a clothes peg. The culprit was finally unmasked.

As the coastal mountains were beginning to fade in the late afternoon a pair of startling clouds formed over the peaks of Kinn and Batalden, two of the outermost high islands. *Hirta*'s stern was directly towards them as she sailed out into the ocean. We had seen these spectacular effects before but now it was obvious how useful they must have been to medieval seamen. They stood out sharply and were obviously going to be visible at a great distance.

Chris and I were discussing this when Mike, who had been too busy with his first-year university examinations to study Norse navigation, joined in the conversation.

'How did the Vikings know which way to go?' he wondered. 'Didn't they use a magnet on a string for a compass – a lodestone, was it?'

'I saw that picture as well,' replied Chris, remembering the well-known painting depicting an intrepid-looking Norseman sailing a stormy sea, consulting his chip of magnetite, 'but I think it's spurious. It certainly is for the period we're interested in. None of our boys had ever heard of a lodestone.'

'So how did they know which was east and west once they were out of sight of land?'

'For a start,' I explained, 'they didn't have points of the compass as such. They used general directions which they called *airts*. There were eight of them. The northern one had its centre under the Pole Star, the southern one middled in way of the sun at noon where shadows were shortest, and the others were estimated between those two.'

'It doesn't sound very accurate to me.'

'Put as baldly as that, I'd agree with you; but what no-one nowadays can understand is that if you've never had a clock or compass and you've spent half your life at sea, your whole sensory perception of time and direction would leave a modern seaman's far behind. Our Norse sea-captain, if he could see the sun at all, would have know perfectly well which *airt* he was steering into. If he could see the Pole Star too, direction was a piece of cake.'

Mike pulled the wheel a couple of spokes to windward. 'He wouldn't do very well tonight then, would he?' he said, gazing astern at the towering orographic island clouds. 'It won't be dark enough to see the Pole Star up here until the end of August.'

'Ah!' broke in Chris. 'That's why they made most of their voyages in spring or autumn. The Pole Star was their only hope on a long trip because without it they were totally lost. If they were on a short passage, say between

116

here and the Faeroes, they simply put something like that cloud astern of them and steered into the correct *airt* until they raised a big mountain near where they were going.'

'What if there were no mountains?' enquired Mike cunningly.

'Fortunately for them there always seem to be this far north,' replied Chris. 'I don't know how they got on in the North Sea, but right up here you could cross the Atlantic without ever being out of sight of land for more than a couple of days. You'd need to have perfect visibility and always make the shortest crossing distance between landfalls, but in theory it's possible.'

Mike nodded thoughtfully, then he looked at the swell which was settling into the new wind direction as it ran down from the vicinity of the North Cape.

'If you noted the relationship between wind direction and sea state each time you had a glimpse of the sun, you'd be able to make a good guess at your heading even if the sky were overcast,' he said, 'and what's more, you'd know when the wind changed and how much because it takes a few hours for the sea to follow it. By the time the sea had come round you'd have a new relationship of ship's head to wind direction and you could start observing afresh. You'd be unlucky if you were far wrong, given a check every day or two . . . especially if you knew the water and you'd been doing it all your life.'

Patrick came up into the cockpit from where he'd been writing at the chart table.

'When I was a kid in Caithness, the older fishermen used to say that they could tell nearly all they needed to know at sea by looking at the birds,' he said. 'There must be other things as well that can help if you know what you're looking for.'

'Whale feeding grounds were certainly used,' I put in. 'About a day's sail south of Iceland there used to be an area that was full of krill. In Viking times the pods of whales dining out were a well-known seamark . . .'

So the talk rambled on into the dog-watch. It seemed that once you began thinking about it, there was any number of possible sources of information about direction and whereabouts, given alert senses and the education to use them. Again the point was powerfully made that the more sophisticated man's mechanical and electronic aids become, the less efficient grow his own sensory functions and his capacity to make deductions from the data they present.

Ros appeared in the companionway carrying the bottle. Hannah followed with her tiny hands full of mugs. It was six o'clock already. Happy Hour. Patrick poured the shots and even John seemed sufficiently recovered to try a small one.

'These short voyages you're on about are all very well,' John began, 'but what really impresses me is the way a *knarr* would sail all the way from

Faeroe

Norway to Greenland without touching land on the way. They couldn't have done that on dead reckoning. They must have had a concept of latitude and a means of measuring distance run. There's no way they could have worked out their north/south position by observing the sun's altitude because that changes with the seasons and you need declination tables to account for it, so they must have used Polaris. It's the only body in the sky that doesn't move at all. It wouldn't be difficult to cobble up something out of wood that could give you the angle between Polaris and the horizon to a degree or so; you could even do it with a stick if you held it vertically a known distance from your eye.

'Suppose you were at sea off Bergen and you noted the altitude of the Pole Star; then when you were at Cape Farewell you found that the altitude was the same, you'd know next time that if you kept it the same all the way and continued sailing west, you'd have to get there sooner or later. You wouldn't be more than fifty miles out at the very worst. It's the age-old system. People have been doing just that for centuries. Do you remember Roger on *Bird of Passage*, Tom?'

I nodded. We'd met him on his little yacht years ago in Spain. He had been bound for the West Indies.

'He crossed the Atlantic like that,' continued John. 'He never could do the sums to work out his longitude. "Latitude, Lead, Log, Look-out and trust in the Lord" he called it. The five L's of navigation. I reckon that's what the Norsemen did. Except they'd have to manage without a log to measure distance and they'd have to trust in Thor instead of our version of the

118

Almighty. They'd certainly have had leadlines to check their depth. What I want to know is what they did for "distance run".'

'I can tell you that,' I offered. 'They were well tuned in to how fast they were sailing, but instead of thinking in miles, and knots or miles per hour, as we do, they thought in terms of an average day's run. I guess for a loaded *knarr* a reasonable figure would be about 120 of our nautical miles. All distances were expressed in this form and it was called a *doegr*.'

Mike pulled on his jacket. 'So you mean that sailing directions for Cape Farewell from Iceland might sound something like this,' he said. '"Sail into the south-west *airt*, leaving Snaefell Glacier behind you. Continue for five *doegr* until you see the high ice-capped mountains. The notch on your stick should now read the same as Bergen"?'

'That's about it,' agreed Chris. 'But there was one hidden extra. These guys nearly always carried a pilot. A fellow like Eirik the Red might have been a useful seafaring man, but he spent too much time feuding and farming ever to be an ace navigator. If he was going somewhere that was well known he would certainly have taken along someone who had been before and who would recognise the land and seamarks.

'The point is that we are spoiled to death because we have charts. If you can't read, and remember, hardly any Vikings could, a chart, even if you had one, wouldn't be much use. There were no charts of Iceland even in the tenth

A turf-roofed farmstead in Faeroe; note the whale jawbones in the foreground

century, let alone Greenland or North America. So you took a pilot. And you treated him well.'

Dinner came and went; the ship settled into her routine of watch and watch, the wind stayed fair and the Atlantic began to open astern of her.

A couple of nights later *Hirta* suffered her only damage of the voyage. Typically, it happened in light weather which is when a ship with heavy gear suffers most. As she rolls there is not enough wind in the rig to steady her and her sailing apparatus bangs about in a most alarming way. Sleep is hard to come by and the vessel is in torment.

The first thing that happened was that one of the two wire-rope topping lifts broke at the turning block at the hounds of the mast. These were the only ropes in the ship that I hadn't replaced for the voyage. I had left them because they were trawl wire with polypropylene fibres woven somehow into their fabric. They had appeared to be in acceptable condition and were way oversize for the job.

As it fell the parted wire brought three heavy blocks down with it. They landed on the deck waking me with the unmistakable sound of problems, but fortunately no-one's head got in their way. Patrick cleared up the mess and he and I discussed what to do about it.

'We could always go into the Faeroes,' he suggested. 'We could find a replacement wire and it'll be simple to reeve a new one off in the calm water.'

I knew Patrick was anxious to call at the Faeroes because all through his boyhood these islands had represented the end of the known world to him and his wee friends as they watched the fishermen come and go. For him it was a place full of romance. It was for me also, but for different reasons. My favourite song for twenty years and more had been Ewan McColl's sympathetic ballad of the herring fishing industry which has so recently passed into history. A few of the many haunting lines go:

> In the stormy seas and the living gale,
> Just to earn our daily bread we're faring,
> From the Dover Strait to the Faeroe Islands
> We've been hunting for the shoals of herring.

What seaman could resist such a call? I tried hard all the same.

'We can manage with just one topping lift, Pat,' I argued. 'We'll sort it out in Iceland.'

At that moment there came a cracking noise from aloft. It came only once but it wasn't healthy. It's only a fool who ignores a warning like that, so we brought out the binoculars and searched the upper mast in the dim light looking for problems. I could see nothing wrong then Patrick spotted it.

'The jib halyard's jumped the sheave on the starboard side.' He pointed to where the halyard passed through one of the seventy-five-year-old original cheek blocks screwed to the side of the spar. The block had pulled away just far enough to allow the rope, which being made of polyester was much smaller than the old hemp one would have been, to slip down between the sheave, or pulley-wheel, and the mast itself. It proved to be jammed solid which was a dangerous situation.

At the change of watch Mike came on deck and as the youngest – and therefore by majority consent, the fittest – he volunteered to go aloft and sort it out. He went up the flimsy ratlines in the sub-Arctic twilight like a monkey and spent what must have been a wretched hour at the top of the wildly swinging mast. Before he left the deck he filled his pockets with shackles, tools, wire and a spare block. Somehow he contrived a working repair. We heard nothing from him except the occasional oath and when he came down he was exhausted. For the only time in his life he tottered straight to the rail and blew his evening meal. Then he sat down in the scuppers and stared at me.

'Why don't we go into the Faeroes, Skipper?' he asked. 'Then we can do a proper job.'

Still I resisted. Time was of considerable importance. We were doing all right, but there was none to waste.

'Just how good is the job up there, Mike?' I wanted to know.

'Oh, it'll do,' he replied, 'but I'd be happier to take another look at it before we tackle Cape Farewell.'

'That's all right then; Iceland next stop.'

Two hours later I was presented with the third hint as John announced the shipping forecast.

'"Deepening Atlantic low south of Iceland, moving steadily north-east, expected north-west of Faeroe Islands by 1300 tomorrow." Westerly gales, Skip. Probably for the next two or three days. Pouring rain. Poor viz. Maybe fog . . .'

John, ever tactful, still didn't offer any gratuitous advice, but then a puffin flew past us in the twilight. He was bang on course for Thorshaven in the Faeroes.

'Do you remember the story of Raven Floki?' asked John as though he hadn't a care in the world.

'Who the devil was he?'

'He was the Viking who wasn't too sharp in the navigation department,' John continued. 'He was on passage from Norway to Iceland and he took three ravens along for the ride. When he was good and lost he let one go and it flew off straight to the eastwards. He ignored that one and let off another a day or so later. That one flew around like a chicken without a head and then came back to the ship. The third day number three went away of its own

(overleaf) Faeroese rowing boats

121

accord and headed a touch north of west. Floki followed it and two days later there he was. A perfect landfall. He was known as Raven Floki ever afterwards.'

'So what?' I asked brusquely. It was long past my bedtime. Also I was distracted from this doubtless fascinating tale by the thought of two days of westerly gales.

'I was just thinking about that puffin,' John commented. 'Maybe we should listen to what we're being told and alter course like Floki did.'

I gave in, and the next morning the grey line of the Faeroe Islands spread across the horizon over our bow.

At eight o'clock Mike and John came on deck to take over the watch. Mike scanned the magnificent mountainous archipelago through his early-morning spectacles and without comment concentrated his attention instead on a pair of puffins. They were flying by at their usual altitude of one foot above sea-level with their ridiculous little wings whirring and their multi-coloured beaks set towards the islands.

'*Hirta* should feel at home in this place,' he said.

'Why's that?' asked John as he took the wheel from Chris.

'Because this is the only known community where they eat as many puffins as they used to on St Kilda. It's puffins for breakfast, dinner and tea up here!'

Mike was referring to the fact that in the 1930s our boat, then with her original name of *Cornubia*, had made so many voyages to the remote fastness of St Kilda that her owner, a well-known Scottish nobleman, had renamed her in honour of the main island of that westernmost outpost of Scotland. The community on Hirta had been disbanded and brought to the mainland before that date but it was quite true that in their day they had been prodiguous consumers of seabirds and seabird eggs.

'I'll tell you something else about puffins,' Mike went on. 'Not only are they tasty and nutritious roasted, boiled, or boned and deep-fried, but they are the farthest-roaming non-pelagic seabird of the northern hemisphere.' Having delivered himself of this surprising headful of information, he added as an afterthought, 'and I'm sure they would make wonderful pets.'

As the islands came closer we became aware of the enormous scale of what we were seeing. From a distance the mountains looked like toys but as we entered the channel that leads up to the town of Thorshavn we began to realise that we were creeping along with shocking slowness like a microscopic bug between a pair of dull green walls of immense height. The sky looked a villainous leaden grey and we were motoring now through ominously still air to get in before the storm broke. The rate of fall of the barometer left no doubt that winds in excess of Force 8 were imminent.

As we powered in Patrick and I were theorising about what sort of bars we could expect in this gutsy bastion of seafaring humanity but as usual Chris, our resident expert on Scandinavian drinking laws, set us straight.

'If you thought Norway was bad,' he began in a voice heavy with resignation, 'this place'll blow you away. The nearest you're allowed to come to enjoying yourself is a Puffin on a Stick. The islands are bone dry.'

Hannah arrived in the cockpit just in time to save Patrick from resorting to blasphemy. Her opening remark left no doubt that someone had been winding her up about our destination and its possibilities.

'Can we really have chocolate-covered puffins in the Fairy Islands, Daddy?' she asked, her eyes wide with wonder as yet another clutch of the impossible birds zipped like clockwork toys close overhead on a bombing run. Ros glowered at Mike who was staring innocently at the end of the bowsprit.

As with all northern harbours there was no charge here for lying alongside the town quay. No sooner were we secured to the dock than the clouds which had been hanging formlessly around since morning organised themselves and began to bowl away towards the north-east in endless procession. The wind picked up and a vile, saturating, misty drizzle came driving down the bleak mountain slopes. By evening it was blowing like a hooligan.

Hirta lay in Thorshavn for a week and it proved to be one of our few stops where we made minimal contact with the local community.

I managed to find some suitable rope for the topping lifts but it turned out to be almost unspliceable and Patrick and Mike spent the whole of an ugly day trying to produce four eyes in its resistant fibres, a job they would normally have run off in an hour or less.

Since all our visits to the shore were made at the double between rainstorms, the impressions they left tend to present themselves in the form of mental snapshots rather than the usual cine film duly edited by the observer's self-defence mechanism: there were the turf-roofed houses, now with plate glass over the old smoke holes but otherwise bearing a strong resemblance to the sort of homes Thorvald Asvaldsson would have seen on his probable stop-over with Eirik on their way to Iceland.

The treeless landscape was a notable feature, and the sad-looking unshorn sheep. Chris and I visited a farm hoping for a quick job shearing to boost our grim-looking bank balance. 'No thank you,' was the answer from the honest farmer who seemed surprised and even alarmed to see us, 'they are all done.' Chris bagged his well-greased shears and my chance of being apprenticed for a couple of days to a real craftsman faded into obscurity.

On the first evening we found a 28ft glassfibre yacht alongside us containing an angelic-looking Swedish professor rejoicing in the name of Lassie, and the fascinating Soffi, his Finnish crew. Like us, they were bound to the westward. Soffi wore so many sweaters that she looked like a French motor-tyre advertisement until one day we all went to the magnificent swimming pool provided for the islanders by the Danish government. The sweaters came off and we understood why Lassie was always smiling.

Soffi gave Hannah two small stones which fitted perfectly into a pair of beautifully knitted mohair bags. 'You heat the stones in the oven till they are too hot to hold,' she explained to the child from temperate England; 'then you pop them in the bags and put one in each pocket. When you are cold, you can warm your hands up by holding them. The heat goes up your arms and soon you are comfy all over.'

Ros restocked the ship at the massively subsidised supermarket in Thorshavn which sold everything except the longed-for puffin cutlets. The prices were so affordable that we were still drinking German coffee a year later that we had bought in the Faeroes. Many Faeroese are disaffected with their Danish overlords and campaign for independence, but the Danes seem at least to do better for their islands than do the British government for their West Indian crown colonies. Roads in these far northern isles are excellent and the mainly fishing economy is well bolstered-up from the outside, giving what appears to be a reasonable standard of living.

We bought fresh fish daily from an old tobacco-chewing Grimsby fisherman who arrived each evening in his beautiful double-ended open boat to sell his catch on the quay. In his youth on the herring boats he had married a Faeroese girl and had left the hurly-burly of the North Sea drifters for the more peaceful life of the islands, but he still had his Humberside voice and we enjoyed his yarns as much as his fish.

One by one we made a pass at the Seamen's Mission where it was rumoured that baths were to be had, and a week after arriving, when the sky, the barometer and the BBC all promised a major improvement in the weather, we decided to water up and leave. Water could only be obtained by jerrycan from the newspaper office on the quay and Mike and Chris disappeared inside this unlikely source of supply carrying the 6 gallon (30 litre) Norwegian battery-acid cans that we now used as water containers. The boys were a long time coming out. Finally they reappeared, red in the face and clearly tipsy.

'I'm not going back in there,' said Chris. 'You go, you'll soon take the point. He's got enough beer in there for the whole island and he's a political activist. He's getting going on the Home Rule theme!'

This seemed too improbable a party to miss so I took the next turn, followed by John who went in with Ros for the final load. They came rollicking back just as Patrick returned from his study of the fishing fleet, to find he had missed the only liquid entertainment of the week.

'It's a shame we're leaving here,' John said. Patrick looked at him quizzically as John went on. 'The best deal you can ever hope for on water is that if you're lucky it'll be free. In Mexico I had to pay for it, and got Montezuma's Revenge into the bargain, but here, not only is it available, it comes with a health guarantee and you get free beer with every canful!'

That night we had a party with Lassie and Soffi and the following morning *Hirta* sailed bravely out of the lee of the island for another bout with the harsh reality of the North Atlantic.

Waves, whales, fog and a Viking landfall

I BELIEVE that as *Hirta* set sail from Thorshavn bound on the next short leg of her Norse Atlantic crossing, all hands probably felt as I did. We were in a wild part of the ocean where gales blew hard and the sea was without pity, yet we were still not outside the great psychological bubble of protection that exists in some mysterious way around Europe. There is another one around North America which extends to the outer islands of the Caribbean and, for some reason, it is possible to sail in these waters without giving yourself the impression that the ancient gods of the sea are being tempted by your enterprise.

It would be impossible to define the root of this sensation that somehow you have not yet severed the umbilical cord with civilisation. It is certainly nothing to do with the presence of effective search-and-rescue services to assist in the event of a catastrophe which is just as likely here as anywhere else. I suspect rather that it is more tied up with the subconscious knowledge that ships have been passing and repassing these waters in considerable numbers over many centuries and that, in consequence, you are somehow not alone.

Once we left Iceland bound towards Cape Farewell and the ice of Greenland, the feeling was no longer present. We were then into the realms of wild adventurers, desperate whaling men and a few dedicated scientific explorers, but on passage from the Faeroe Islands up to Iceland we still sailed in the unseen company of countless fishermen and over a thousand years of regular trade.

Certainly in Eirik the Red's day the Norse seafaring community would have entertained similar intimations of confidence or foreboding. A trader, or even a settler like Eirik's father, setting forth towards Iceland from Thorshavn would have known in his heart that he was sailing well-travelled water. Even though he had never heard of a chart or a compass, he was confident that so many others had made the journey successfully that he should be able to do the same. For Eirik himself, and for those who followed after on the voyages to Greenland and beyond, the cold impersonal neutrality of that vast sea virtually unpassed by man must have been a tangible thing. It

127

is easy to say that one chunk of ocean is pretty much like another, but in a mystical way this is not so. Some of us felt the difference, and if it was clear to us with our diesel engine, our charts, our chronometers and our certain knowledge that the world is round, how much stronger it must have been for tenth-century men in real touch with the environment.

Our dangerously casual approach to the five-hundred-mile passage was exchanged in short order for a sharp reminder that we were in latitude 62°N and that we weren't on a pleasant summer yachting jaunt. The BBC had issued a forecast of southerly winds of Force 3 or 4 with fog banks. Since we expected soon to clear the land and also any shipping that might be around, fog presented little hazard, so we hoisted the full main and the big jib (repaired in Norway) with high hopes, and bore away to the westward into the Skopunar fjord which leads between two islands to the western ocean.

If sea conditions for leaving Norway after the previous gale had been poor, the state of affairs in the Skopunar fjord needed to be seen to be believed. The only thing going for *Hirta* was the tide which was due to set to the westward until bedtime.

Colossal cliffs towered into the clouds on both sides of us. The rain soaked us through in a matter of minutes. The wind, so peacefuly forecast, was blasting straight up and down the pass with devilish strength at a minimum of Force 6 and gusting up to gale force. The sea itself looked like nothing on earth. Great mountains of water were rearing up indiscriminately all over the place as the swell left by a week of heavy weather tried to power itself through the narrow gulf. As the waves smashed into the cliffs the spray was hurled into the clouds where it mixed with the rain. It was an apocalyptic scene.

One thing was clear; we had to reduce sail immediately. Where to start was the question, but this wasn't in doubt for long. *Hirta* fell off a brutally steep wave, and buried her whole lee deck in solid water. She was being overpowered utterly by the foretriangle and the jib looked like going the same way as it had gone just north of the Sognefjord.

'Roll up the jib, John,' I suggested. 'If it blows out again it'll only be good for patching jeans.'

'Are you sure you wouldn't like to start again tomorrow?' asked Chris. 'That newspaper editor's still got heaps of good cheer left.'

I ignored this irrelevance and ran *Hirta* square off the wind so that the sail, which was pulling like a team of horses, would be blanketed by the mainsail and the boys would have a chance to furl it. As soon as the boat was on a dead run the jib collapsed in defeat in the wind shadow and John and Chris had it rolled away in a trice. As I brought the boat back to the wind to beat on under main and staysail Mike appeared carrying the spitfire jib. With Herculean efforts the foredeck men changed the sails in spite of being drenched by solid seawater. We then hove to in mid-channel and reefed the main.

Now *Hirta* was rigged to handle the conditions and tack by tack, she punched her way out into the Atlantic, smashing unstoppably through the impossible seas while the hands collapsed in a saturated, worn-out heap in the cockpit.

Then came the fog. It had already occurred to me that the cloudbase, which was extremely low, didn't have to drop much more to envelop us completely, and that is what now happened. One minute it was pouring with rain and the clouds were tearing by just above the masthead, and the next, we were in dense fog and the rain was replaced by what Mike described as megadrizzle. Ten minutes afterwards, just as I was becoming concerned as to our position in relation to the awesome cliffs, the wind freed to the southward and we were able to lay the course out of the fjord with our sheets eased.

Chris was steering a compass course now, instead of guiding the ship to windward by watching the sails and by feel.

'You remember all that theorising we were doing about how the Vikings knew what course they were steering?' he asked rhetorically. 'All I can say is, I'm damn glad I've got a compass in front of me now. The wind's backed 50° while I've been on the helm but the sea is so disorganised by all these cliffs and islands you'd never know by relating the two. The way things are, we won't see anything else until we reach Iceland.'

While we were pondering the undoubted truth of these observations. Hannah appeared from down below carrying a bucket containing something not very pleasant.

'My bear's been sick,' she announced.

'Must have been something he ate.'

'More likely something he had too much of in the newspaper office!'

'Well, don't just stand there, throw it over the side.'

'Look out!'

'Hang on!'

'OH NO!' *Hirta* stood on her bowsprit as a peculiarly square wave got in her way and Chris copped the whole bucketful in the lap of my Number Two oilskins, his own having been left on the dump in the Faeroes. He looked at the mess in disgust, then scowled at Hannah.

'It's every bear for himself now,' he began with murder in his eyes. 'You tell him . . . aaargh!' and he disappeared under half a ton of abrasive seawater that climbed aboard over the quarter. The rest of us saw it coming and jumped for shelter but Chris had been too busy considering his misery to maintain a proper awareness of the sea state.

'Nice of you to clean the skipper's oilies so thoroughly,' said Mike as the water drained out of Chris' trouser bottoms.

A broad reach and a strong breeze
(*opposite*) *Rigging service*

After this rough start, things rapidly improved. The fog hung around but the wind blew steadily from the southwards and by midnight *Hirta* was rattling up the miles towards Reykjavik. The following day we began to sight whales. The first few we saw were all well away and were recognisable only by their spouts and the odd gracefully-turning single-finned back. On the third day out, however, John roused us with a 'Thar she blows!' Then he added more quietly, 'right under the quarter, in fact.' We all tumbled out to enjoy a memorable encounter.

Hirta was sailing at about 5 knots in an easy sea and just astern to port was an adult finback whale. He was fully as long as the ship and as he swam easily just outside the small disturbance created by our passage he rolled slightly to allow his eye to check us over. The eyes of this type of whale are situated abaft the inner end of the huge mouth which seems to be on the wrong part of the head, being in its upper section rather than the lower.

We could see his blow-hole working and hear the mighty rush of air as he exhaled periodically. Had we been of a belligerent frame of mind he was more than close enough to harpoon, but for a cumbersome creature like twentieth-century man who needs to make a boat in order to survive even moderate ocean conditions, to even contemplate doing violence to one of the great mysteries of creation must surely be unthinkable.

130

It is always a salutary experience to come alongside a whale in mid-ocean because the meeting rubs one's nose into the hard fact that all man has going for him is a brain, and for the most part he hasn't grown up enough even to handle that very well. In contrast, the whale is in perfect harmony with his environment. He does not struggle to alter his surroundings because he has adapted to them superbly, freeing his not inconsiderable mind for, who knows, perhaps better things.

After a stay of ten minutes or so, our visitor blew for the last time, threw his gigantic tail twenty feet in the air and disappeared into the deep, leaving us strangely silent, feeling small in more ways than one.

Ros looked at the slick left by his final sounding. 'It makes you feel presumptuous, doesn't it?' she said quietly.

And that about summed it up.

On the 'night' of the fourth day out of Thorshavn visibility was again poor. It was too long since we had seen the sun to be sure of our position and so we tried a fix with our radio-direction-finding (RDF) set. This old-fashioned device is of limited usefulness but it is *Hirta*'s only concession to electronic navigational aids. Compared with the modern hyperbolic and satellite systems installed in many yachts on both sides of the Atlantic, it is primitive and unsure, but in circumstances where there has been no astronomical observation for days, it is all we have with which to check our dead reckoning. It only works in fairly close proximity to a series of transmitting stations which is another limitation, but even so, it's more than Eirik the Red had.

This fix put us alarmingly close to the coast of southern Iceland, of which the *Arctic Pilot* has this to say, '. . . there is no habitation of any kind in this area except for a few isolated farms on the south-west bank of Kúdhafljot . . .' Mariners are then advised that the coast is dangerous to shipping and that 'the crews of stranded ships are almost certain to undergo severe privations. To reach Vik, 7 miles west of Kötlutangi, means crossing many rivers and in conditions of low visibility a local guide is essential.'

A close inspection of the coastal chart showed the sites of various refuge huts apparently put there specifically for shipwrecked sailors, all of which presented an unpromising picture for the crews of vagrant pilot cutters unsure of their position, so we hove to on the offshore tack to await a better view.

The following morning the sun came out and we verified our whereabouts. We needn't have worried. We were nearer our dead reckoning position than we were to the radio fix, but that afternoon all speculation about my sextant work was brought to a glorious halt when we were given the benefit of a fine Viking landfall.

'I've been watching that cloud bank up to the northward for an hour now,' said John as Mike took over the helm at Happy Hour, 'and I've noticed that the upper part of it is very white and it is not changing its shape at all. Could it be a glacier?'

I dived down to the chart table and worked out the bearing of Myrdalsjokul, the most likely candidate, from our estimated position. Then I passed John the handbearing compass to check his mountain. The two coincided perfectly. We had found Iceland in the traditional way. If we'd had no radio to confuse us we'd have raised the high land that morning just the same. If we'd had the benefit of a good Norse pilot, he'd have known straightaway what it was and what was our distance off.

In fair weather and twenty-four hour daylight now, we began cruising around the south-west coast of Iceland. Twelve hours later we passed between Surtsey, the island created by a volcanic upheaval in 1963, and the inner members of the Westman group. These islands were named by the ninth-century Norse colonists of Iceland after the Irish monks and Anchorites, known to them as Westmen, who inhabited the land before they arrived. Considerable numbers of these unfortunates were driven to their deaths over the fearful cliffs of the islands that bear their name. If you believe the official saga version of the story, the suggestion is that all those thus executed were revolting slaves foully guilty of murdering their poor, defenceless masters. However, it seems just as likely that the Celts were quietly minding their own business on these secluded rocks when along came the Vikings in search of fun. Priest-bashing was always a favourite pastime; the rest of the story can be imagined.

Hirta rounded the smoky headland of Reykjaness at midnight and we could smell the sulphur from the volcanic activity as we swept by. Later that day we sailed into the crowded inner harbour at Reykjavik with everything up, including our topsail. I suppose we were expecting the town crier to turn out, or something of that sort, but the harbour was full of activity of all kinds and no-one took the slightest notice of us.

We berthed in amongst some inshore fishing craft underneath what appeared to be a transport cafe with picture windows. The diners all took a casual glance in our direction and then re-addressed themselves to the consumption of the crispy cod balls that none of us could ever afford to sample.

John and I were putting a harbour stow on the mainsail when he looked at the western sky and voiced my own thoughts.

'Plenty of cirrus up there, Skip. Looks like we just made it again.' At that moment a vicious gust of wind blew a cloud of dust over us from the vicinity of the transport cafe, and Ros poked her head up from down below.

'Tea's up, boys,' she announced, and then added as an afterthought. 'Have you noticed the barometer? It's dropped ten points in the last four hours!'

Mike checks out Surtsey – which is the same age as he is

Hirta follows Eirik's
ill-fated migration

TEN centuries before *Hirta* carried her topsail proudly into the heart of Reykjavik, Eirik the Red's travel-stained *knarr* had sailed into the next great bay to the north returning from her three-year voyage of exploration. She was bleeding traces of rust from her iron fastenings and her sail was heavily patched with the rough repairs sailors have always called 'homeward bounders'. The golden colour of her oiled planking was blackened by the hardest use in the world, but her hold was packed with the wealth of the sea.

As for Eirik and his men, they stepped ashore to greet the stay-at-homes with that special swagger that is peculiar to seamen at the conclusion of a lengthy voyage. Their hands and faces were weathered with the wind and salt so that superficially they appeared to have aged more than the thousand days of their exile. Their long wind-tangled hair framed eyes that retained for days, or even weeks, the distant look of the man who has been to the end of the world. Their women and their old allies no doubt rejoiced to see them safely home, and both parties must have been hungry for news, the main item of which on the home front was that Thorgest of Breidabolstead was still spoiling for a fight.

As soon as Eirik learned that his stubborn adversary had neither forgiven nor forgotten the events of three years past, he must have made his decision. He had had plenty of time to consider his options and, by now, the idea of being the founding father of a brand new colony was probably so attractive to him that he was glad of the excuse offered by the promise of further aggravation. His days in Iceland were definitely over and he let it be known that the following year he intended to return to the new land he had taken on the far side of Cape Farewell. It was the autumn of the year 984 and Eirik was in his middle thirties.

It was not a part of Eirik's plans that he and his family should creep away to the south-west and live out their days in secret exile. On the contrary, he must have systematically leaked the news of his intentions as far and wide as he could so as to drum up support for the enterprise. Although some of the coast he had discovered was of a quality at least comparable to the less choice farming districts of Iceland, the general atmosphere of the place and the obvious proximity of a permanent icecap were going to make it difficult to sell. Undeterred by this problem and unfettered by a 'christian' conscience he laid an early precedent on behalf of the real estate agents of future generations. In the words of Eirik's saga: 'He named it [the country] *Greenland*, for he said that people would be much more tempted to go there if it had an attractive name.'

It was a shrewd move, and all that winter enquiries came flocking in to the home of Ingolf, where Eirik had been accepted as a house-guest pending his final departure.

There were plenty of reasons why Eirik's scheme was finding popular acclaim: Iceland had been inhabited by Norsemen for a hundred years by this time and was becoming, by the standards of the day, somewhat overcrowded. The fact that a chief like Eirik's father had been forced to settle for an obscure second-rate holding testifies to this, and many a man who perhaps lacked Eirik's initiative or opportunities would have cheerfully signed on in the hope of improving his state. A large proportion of the original settlers of Iceland were hard men from Norway with a history of being quick to avenge an insult, whether it were real or imaginary. Thousands of such folk thrown together in a land of limited agricultural possibilities led to countless incidents of the type which had resulted in the banishment of Eirik himself. For a considerable number of her inhabitants Iceland had already become a dangerous place with no certain future except a final encounter with cold iron. A further reason for discontent was the steady infiltration of Christianity. The new religion was proving attractive to the ladies, and the threat of holy communion and other such intolerable goings-on in his own hall must have provided further motivation for a man to move house, and take his womenfolk as far as he could from the lily-livered but subversive priests.

Not all Eirik's converts were malcontents or people with financial difficulties. Several characters of high esteem also began to sell up their excess property and commission ships for the voyage to Greenland. Even the well-known trader, Herjolf Bardarson, came along. Herjolf's family had been in Iceland as long as anybody could remember. His grandfather had visited the place with Raven Floki, the famous bird-flyer, on one of the first-ever Norse voyages to the west. This elder Herjolf had shown a remarkable perception that he passed on to his progeny because Raven Floki had not considered Iceland worth settling! Herjolf reckoned differently and had grabbed the first opportunity to return and stake his claim. Now his grandson was away once more on the long road westward.

When spring came to the wide waters of Breidafjord there were at least twenty-five ships fitting out to sail for Cape Farewell. It is impossible not to marvel at the magnetism of Eirik the Red. He had walked into Haukadale not so long ago as the owner of a poor, northern farmstead and was now ready to put to sea at the head of what was, by any telling, a substantial fleet of ships containing within their boards the future of many hundreds of virile people.

Before he was prepared to sail, however, Eirik had still to clear up the persistent unpleasantness with Thorgest. There is no record of who instigated the final showdown but some time in the spring of 985 a pitched battle was fought between the two adversaries and their supporters. Eirik had his usual crowd of faithful followers and the powerful Thord Bellower had tossed his hand in alongside Thorgest. The result of this confrontation put the final cap on Eirik's decision-making process. If there had remained even a vestige of doubt in his mind about the wisdom of going off to Greenland, this final set-to removed it for all time.

He lost.

None of the principal contenders was gravely injured in the fight, but afterwards Eirik, who probably wished to depart in good odour so as to encourage trade with his new land, made a deal with Thorgest and they were legally reconciled. What they thought of one another personally must be unprintable but both were hard-headed enough to see that there was no future in carrying on as they had been for the last few years.

Having completed this final business Eirik set sail as the days lengthened into summer and was soon followed by the rest of the fleet. He was clear enough about the exact location of Cape Farewell to be able to issue the other shipmasters with adequate sailing directions to make the passage direct although several members of Eirik's original crew must surely have been employed by the more well-to-do as specialist pilots. Before leaving, many of the crews propitiated Thor or the individual god of their choice. Herjolf Bardarson, however, had shipped a Christian from the Hebrides who was probably the family saga-writer, or *skald*. This man braved the head-shaking and axe-rattling of the reactionaries and is on record as having offered a prayer to Jesus on behalf of all hands. It went like this:

I beseech the immaculate monk-seeker
To give us a good voyage.
May the King of Heaven's Halls
Hold his hand over me.

With this controversial benediction ringing in his ears, Herjolf squared away his great sail and drove out of Breidafjord towards his destiny. As the north-east wind took him past the proximity of Snaefelsness and he put the unmistakable mountain astern, he set his ship's head into the western portion of the south-west *airt* and relaxed his mind to run his five *doegr*. Abeam and astern of him the other *knarrs* dipped and rolled, their masts backstayed strongly and their sails pulling like hunting hounds at the leash. As the livestock jostled in the ship's waist and his people crowded the steering platform so that the fainthearts could gaze weakly astern, the only question mark in Herjolf's mind must have concerned his son, Bjarni.

Bjarni was the same age as Eirik Thorvaldsson, and from early childhood had shown nothing but promise as a sailor. As he grew up he developed in addition considerable ability in the second great Viking attribute, that of buying and selling. These two skills, coupled with the sort of nature which did not attract trouble had made him a rich man and this summer, as was his custom every other year, he was on passage to Iceland from Norway with a cargo of trade goods. When he arrived at Herjolf's hall it would be empty but Herjolf had left instructions so that, if he had a mind to, Bjarni could follow the older man down to the virgin ground of Greenland. And so, wondering if he would see his son again, this steadfast old Viking steered on in the wake of Eirik the Red.

Not many weeks after Herjolf's departure Bjarni arrived home ready for a winter doing business around the farms in Iceland. His father's message was waiting for him, but already it was apparent that for many of the colonists the voyage to the promised land had been a shambles, while for others, it seemed likely to have been a fatal disaster.

Along the shores of Faxafloi and Breidafjord lay *knarrs* with broken masts, stove in boards and ruined cargoes. They sat high and dry on the beaches in pitiful disarray with the morale of their surviving crews shattered.

Halfway between Iceland and Cape Farewell, the fleet had been struck by the dreaded *hafgerdingar* – the Whirling Sea. The *hafgerdingar* was not a normal storm, it was a more mysterious phenomenon which we in the twentieth century can probably put

138

*Mysterious conditions near Thingvellir, Iceland, site of
the* Althing; *a tern fishes the still lake water in the grey
afternoon while a hot spring steams vigorously in the
background*

down to some huge volcanic eruption on the seabed. Such terrible
waves were rarely reported by the hard-bitten Norsemen who were
not prone to exaggeration and the *hafgerdingar* was certainly not a
matter of legend. When it struck, few survived to tell the tale . . .

'SO what exactly is it that we can do for you?' enquired
Dr Thor Jakobsson of the Sea Ice Division in his cosy
office at the modern Icelandic Weather Station. The
station stands on high ground in the outskirts of Reykjavik, and on the
morning of this, the first of our many visits, the rain was lashing the
windows and the south-west gale was threatening to blow the place clean off
its rock.

Dr Jakobsson is a neatly-turned-out man of slim build and a little under
average height. Patrick and I towered over him feeling extremely hairy. Our

139

Number One shore-going rigs seemed scruffy in his presence, but mercifully he was not interested in our appearance.

'We are from the old English cutter in the harbour,' I explained, 'and we are on passage from Norway to Newfoundland. Our intention is to call at Eiriksfjord in southern Greenland on the way if it's possible. But we have no specific ice information, only the general monthly charts. Can you bring us up to date with the current position?'

'Yes, we will be happy to do that,' he replied, 'but first I will explain the general movement of ice in the area you will be entering.' Then suddenly he asked, quite out of context. 'Are you the ship that is following the Norse westward voyages?' I glanced at Patrick. He was gaping in amazement. Was there no privacy at all in the North Atlantic? We hadn't yet spoken to a soul in Iceland. I nodded dumbly at the good doctor. 'I thought so,' he continued. 'I had a communication from the British Met Office at Bracknell that you might be calling. You were there in April asking about general conditions. Yes?'

'Yes,' I replied, astonished that these highly skilled scientists whose forecasts might one day decide the fate of nations could take the slightest interest in an operation like ours.

Dr Jakobsson, however, was clearly delighted by our visit, 'Then you know the basic situation about the south Greenland ice,' he said. 'The coast is completely icebound in the winter but the pack starts to break up in May and June. As it comes free from the coast it moves south down the east side of the country on the East Greenland Current, then it hooks around Cape Farewell and drifts northwards into Baffin Bay until it meets with the south-flowing Labrador Current which runs right down to the Grand Banks off Newfoundland.

'By late July the coast you are interested in around what is now Julianehaab may be clear of ice, but there is often a tongue of pack ice which extends to the north-westward from Cape Farewell for hundreds of miles. In order to enter the Julianehaab Bight where Eiriksfjord is situated, you would need to sail around this. In fair weather that would present no problems, but if you got inside the ice into the shore-lead and there was a heavy onshore gale, you could be trapped between the ice and shore. Is your ship protected with ice plates?'

'No,' I replied, remembering the iron sheets nailed neatly around the bow of the old Baltic Trader on which John, Ros and I had met.

'Hmm . . .' said Thor Jakobsson.

'Would we be right in thinking that by August we could enter the fjords in an average year with no real fears from heavy ice?' asked Patrick, for this had been our impression from the English meteorologists.

'Yes, that is quite true,' he mused, 'but by late August the weather is beginning to turn bad. You have a narrow window in the general conditions, and you are reliant on a reasonable ice situation. Of course, if you were going further north, to Godthaab for example, where the old Norse so-called western settlement was sited, things would be much simpler for you.'

'Unfortunately, we're not,' I replied, wishing to goodness that we were. 'It's too far up there for the time available. We need to get down to the United States before the winter gales set in so we have been relying on average conditions.'

'Hmm . . .' said Dr Jakobsson again. I was beginning to wish he'd get to the point. 'I'm afraid you have picked a bad year, gentlemen,' he finally admitted producing North Atlantic ice charts for yesterday like a conjuror. 'It is now mid-July. You see we have heavy pack ice still fifty miles south of Cape Farewell and the Julianehaab Bight is blocked solid. The ice in East Greenland last winter was the worst for a hundred years.'

'What about the weather systems?' asked Patrick, seemingly undeterred by this doomsday announcement.

The meteorologist looked sheepish, then he flipped another chart out of a folio on his desk. 'More bad news, I'm sorry,' he mumbled. 'There is a very strong high pressure system over England. They are having the finest summer for twenty years. This means the polar front is displaced from its usual position and the depressions are running straight from Nova Scotia through Iceland. The weather is terrible. My wife is sick and tired of it . . . Ah well,' he shrugged relaxing once more into his weatherman's fatalism, 'what we cannot change, we must accept. Come! Have some lunch with me.'

He led us into the dining room where we enjoyed a perfect summer lunch on what looked for all the world like a January day. Afterwards we toddled off, accepting with gratitude the suggestion that we return for more up-to-date information after a few days.

As it was Friday and, according to the meteorologists, nothing much was open over the weekend, Patrick and I decided to try our luck at the Reykjavik *Vinmonopole* on our way back to the ship. I had reservations about the place, but Patrick was keen to have the experience and besides, as he pointed out, the crew would need a morale booster when they heard the weather report, and we needed a change from *Hirta*'s bonded Scotch.

The *Vinmonopole* is rather like a warehouse as you approach it, except that numbers of furtive figures dressed anonymously are entering and leaving carrying plain brown paper bags.

'Look at the guy over there,' Patrick indicated a middle-aged business man who was creeping out of a side door. 'The last time I saw anyone behaving like that he was coming out of the sex shop in Tunbridge Wells!'

*(overleaf) Chris and Mike set foot on 'The Great
Gromboolian Plain' in central Iceland*

141

'He's terrified somebody's going to recognise him, that's why,' I observed. 'This place must be worse than Norway for drink problems. Chris and Mike said that last night they couldn't find a beer in the whole of Reykjavik. There is no beer. What do you think of that?'

'Sounds like a formula for violent crime on a massive scale,' retorted the Scottish ex-soldier. 'Why can't any of these people cope with the booze? Is it something to do with the latitude, or are they afraid that if they relax the laws the whole population will go on a ten-year bender and die of alcoholism?' We carried the discussion no further because by then we were in through the front door.

In front of us a counter of immense length stretched into the distance like a young artist's exercise in perspective drawing. On one side of it was a scrummage of Icelanders clutching their pay packets, and on the other a band of dedicated men were serving up the bottles. We soon discovered to our delight that imported wine was only a fraction more costly than at home.

'We'd better load up on claret!' I said to Patrick who was standing firm while a desperate queue-jumper bounced off his powerful chest.

'There'll be no shortage of that' he said, squinting through the bodies to check what everyone was buying. 'All these folks are stocking up on spirits. They cost a fortune. I don't understand why they aren't getting in the wine.'

'I wonder if that stuff they are grabbing in the dark bottles is what Chris was talking about – the Black Death?'

It was.

As we strolled back to the ship we noticed that many of the shops were boarding up their windows. The casual way they were doing the job suggested that this was a normal Friday night precaution.

After dinner we were all sitting on deck when we noticed a pair of tough-looking policemen on Harley-Davidsons watching us. Ros and I wandered across to admire the bikes and soon we were yarning with the strong arm of the law. They, like everyone else here, spoke our language, so that once again we were humbled at the arrogance of the English-speaking nations on the question of learning foreign tongues.

For a while we discussed motorcycles, pilot cutters, Eirik the Red and the best place to hire a car to go to Thingvellir; then one policeman looked at his watch.

'9.30.' He winked knowingly at his mate. 'It'll start soon.'

'What'll start soon?' enquired Ros innocently.

'You'll see!'

We talked on. Hannah, who should have been asleep, hopped ashore in her Wee Willie Winkie nightie; the cop hoisted her playfully and sat her like a mascot on the tank of his Harley. Mike, like me a motorcycle fanatic, sauntered over and joined in. It was a pleasant, civilised scene. The wind had dropped for a while and the sun was up so that it was almost warm enough to be without a padded jacket.

Suddenly, from the depths of the town, came a bloodcurdling scream followed by miscellaneous shouts and the crash of breaking glass. One policeman grinned broadly at the other, then at Ros.

'So you see; now it has started,' he chuckled as he lowered Hannah gently to the tarmac and revved up his monster bike. 'Friday is the only night we have any fun.'

The second guardian of the peace pulled on his gauntlets and flexed his knuckles significantly. Then, smirking from ear to ear in anticipation of an evening's action, he let in his clutch and the riders roared off to join the fray.

When we climbed back down to *Hirta* Chris was sitting in the cockpit and the noise of casual violence from the town was building up.

'If Eirik the Red could have signed up those two as well as Thorbjorn Vifilsson and the rest, I don't think Thord Bellower and Thorgest would have stood a dog's chance,' he said. 'Then perhaps Eirik wouldn't have bothered going to Greenland and we'd all have been saved a lot of trouble.'

Chris had studied the weather chart, and he had enough imagination to foresee what lay in store.

⤙⟋

That weekend we hired a car and drove off down the dirt roads to visit Thingvellir, the site of the *Althing* where the council of all Iceland had met annually in the tenth century, and where the members of the Thorsness Thing had sat to discuss the case of Eirik (the Red) Thorvaldsson and Thorgest of Breidabolstead.

As we travelled on we inspected some of the modest tracts of farmland which the country offers and began to understand why there had been plenty of takers a thousand years before for a new world called Greenland. Everywhere, away from the farmsteads, lie considerable areas of volcanic desert with sharp spectacular mountains and great glaciers as a backdrop. If you were not at the head of the line when land came vacant, tenth-century Iceland must have been an unforgiving place for a settler.

The Iceland of the twentieth century was an unforgiving place for hire cars and we soon realised why we had been charged a price that had seemed a cynical rip-off when we had dipped into our boots to pay up. Once outside Reykjavik, made-up roads stop and the traveller uses only a variety of dirt tracks. The best of these are well-graded and work adequately if you don't mind the dust, but as our condemned vehicle lurched in resignation up to what Chris, still with *The Jumblies* on his mind, described as the 'great Gromboolian Plain', we felt that if the car lasted six months its corpse would

(overleaf) Ros beside the Gulfos waterfall in Iceland

145

be a credit to its oriental manufacturer.

Back in Reykjavik the following week we began to make daily visits to the weather station. The news was invariably bad. After a brief improvement the low pressure systems began once again to run straight up our track bringing with them westerly gales, rain and fog. The ice stayed put around Cape Farewell and we continued to trudge up and down the hill to see Dr Jakobsson. In the end, the meteorologists became so sorry for us that they started to send a car down to pick us up so that we didn't have to walk in order to receive the hard word. They were also more than generous with their lunches, and Patrick and I gathered a whole sheaf of ice charts, each giving the same miserable message.

And all the time our window on Greenland was closing.

After we had been ten days in Iceland there had been so little summer that the general public staged a full-scale demonstration with banners, placards and chanting outside the Met Office. We took the hint. Perhaps it was us who were the Jonahs. If so, we'd better take the rubbish with us, but even if we weren't, we had no time to wait any longer.

The day after the demonstration, Thor Jakobsson himself came down to *Hirta* with the latest information and plenty of sound advice about what was left for us to do.

'Here is the situation,' he began as he unrolled his charts on the saloon table. 'The ice at Cape Farewell and Eiriksfjord is overdue for moving, but it is unlikely to break up properly until there is a change in the wind. A north-easter for a few days would do wonders.'

'It would do wonders for us, too,' said John, who like the rest of us was concerned about what had happened to the fair winds we were hoping to enjoy in these high latitudes. 'What's the story on the High over England?'

'It is still glorious sunshine in London,' Jakobsson apologised as a heavy shower of rain thudded onto the deck. 'There is no change. If you go now you will start your voyage by sailing straight down the polar front, but for the next two days you have some reasonably gentle winds coming. The next depression is currently off Nova Scotia, but it will bring winds of only Force 6 or so.'

'Are you sure about that?' I asked. 'Maybe we should make a start and take pot luck on the ice.'

'A weatherman is never sure,' Thor Jakobsson smiled sadly. 'We can only predict on the data we have at the moment. Perhaps you can speak with a ship nearer to Cape Farewell and get an up-date, although there are not many ships down there. More likely you will see no-one at all. But you can take hope. A thousand years ago Bjarni Herjolfsson picked up a powerful north-easter when he was bound for Greenland and it blew him all the way to America. Maybe you will have his luck!'

But we didn't . . .

Greenland Sea storms lead Bjarni to discover America

THE news of his father's unexpected emigration came as a shock to Bjarni Herjolfsson, though the initial effect on him and his crew must have been one of anticlimax.

Bjarni subscribed to the usual arrangement of the Icelandic/ Norwegian trader in that he loaded up in Iceland in the spring and sailed to Norway. He then passed the winter in Norway selling his goods and restocking his ship with gear that would fetch a good price at home, voyaging back to Iceland with it the following summer. The next winter was spent trading in Iceland before repeating the cycle.

When his deep-loaded *knarr* fetched up in Iceland in the summer of 985 her arrival was the culmination of a two-year voyage, with all that that means. In addition to anticipating pay-day, Bjarni and his men were looking forward to being re-united with their loved ones and seeing how affairs had proceeded in their absence. For Bjarni, Herjolf's departure meant not only a personal disappointment but also raised questions concerning the future of the shorebased side of his business. In addition, he had reason to be worried about his father's safety. From the news that was coming through it appeared that many of the emigrants had not completed their journey in one piece. Herjolf's *knarr* was not among those that had survived the *hafgerdingar* and limped home, so either she had made it through, or she was now lying at the bottom of the Greenland Sea.

Bjarni saw quickly that he could take one of two alternative courses of action. Either he could write his father off as having gone soft in the head and followed that lunatic Eirik the Red to only

149

Thor knew where, or he could sail west after the colonists with his ship and his trade goods. It seems likely that in his note to his son Herjolf included some words of encouragement about the benefits of keeping the family concern together. If Bjarni made it to the new colony with his ship-load of goodies from the homeland, the Greenlanders would surely be ready to pay top prices for them. Iceland would see several ships from Norway that autumn all offering their wares in the market place and subject to the normal economics of price competition. For the Greenland colonists however, a lean and luxury-free winter lay ahead. Their own ships would have been filled to the waterways with the hard-core necessities for homesteading but even these were in short supply.

Bjarni and Herjolf stood to make a killing.

A man of Bjarni's business acumen cannot have vacillated long over such a decision and, rather than unload the *knarr*, he put his thoughts to the crew for their consideration. The Vikings preferred to run their deep-sea vessels with a limited degree of democracy. There were a variety of excellent reasons for this, the two main ones being that in the first place a Viking with a share of the action was a Viking more likely to pull his weight. The second point was that, because of the ever-present need for self-defence against rogue longships full of pirates, all Norse vessels were overmanned by our standards. If you found yourself in a fight and your ship was crewed by slaves, it was more than possible that your interests and theirs would not run along the same lines and you could end your last voyage in a small and downtrodden minority.

To a man, Bjarni's shipmates voted to go with him to Greenland. That they did so in the face of the inevitable tongue-clicking and head-shaking from the usual gang of Job's comforters on the dock is a tribute to Bjarni's leadership. The crowd on his *knarr* were not just a few out-of-work Vikings dredged up from the bars of Bergen and Trondheim; they were a tried and tested team. He may have tempted them with promises of better profits farther on, or perhaps he threatened them with the old chestnut so beloved of nineteenth-century ship-owners — 'no voyage completion discharge papers, no pay' — but most probably, they were simply a tight ship and a happy crew content to stick together. Above all, they were professionals.

Once all hands had reorganised themselves and the *knarr* was fitted out afresh, Bjarni waited patiently for a fair wind. In his day there was no ice to worry about on this passage and, in due course, nature sent him the pleasant easterly he had awaited and which he had every right to expect.

Away they went until Snaefell Glacier sank beneath the horizon.

For three more days and three nights the fair wind held, as Bjarni had been reasonably certain it would. Now they were entering the latitudes where, in late summer, the twilight deepens into darkness and Bjarni knew he hadn't much farther to sail before he had run his distance. There was no suggestion of a repeat performance from the *hafgerdingar* as the *knarr* creaked, dipped and surged along before the fine passage-making wind. Then as the third twenty-four-hour period out of sight of land drew to its close, the weather bit back at them; 985 was turning out to be 'one of those years'.

The easy sailing breeze backed steadily into the north and it came on to blow. Fog drove down on the gale and soon Bjarni was faced with the matter of handling his ship through a serious storm. All navigational considerations went, so to speak, out the porthole.

At sea, there are various degrees of heavy weather, the worst being the survival storm. What exactly the wind force and sea state of a survival storm may be depends upon whether the unhappy mariner caught by it is in a 10,000-ton motor ship or a 10ft rowing dinghy, but whatever sort of vessel he is sailing, her limitations will soon become clear. In a regular gale a well-found sailing boat of the size of a *knarr* can generally continue to make some way towards her destination, wind direction permitting, but if conditions become really bad, the only consideration left in the skipper's mind will be that of keeping her afloat and undamaged.

The last-ditch options have always varied with the type of vessel; questions of hull shape, draught, beam and weight distribution are important, together with the capacity of the ship's pumps and whether or not she is full decked.

A 50ft deep-draught pilot cutter can heave-to under minimum canvas and lose little ground. If the wind becomes so strong that she can no longer carry any sail at all she can even lie a'hull: that is, simply lie to the sea with no sails up and take what is coming. The danger of this practice is that there is a possibility that the ship may be rolled over by a wave. Deep, heavy craft resist this strongly, but if they do go over, their decks should keep out the water long enough to give them a chance to self-right.

A *knarr*, by comparison, has minimal draught and she is not fully decked; she also has no pumps, just a lot of dedicated Norsemen with buckets. The best way for her to survive a heavy storm must be to run before the wind, presenting her stern to the seas and lessening their force. Bjarni would have had recourse to these tactics on many previous occasions, and that, not surprisingly, is what he did this time.

Driving away under bare poles would keep him afloat: it would

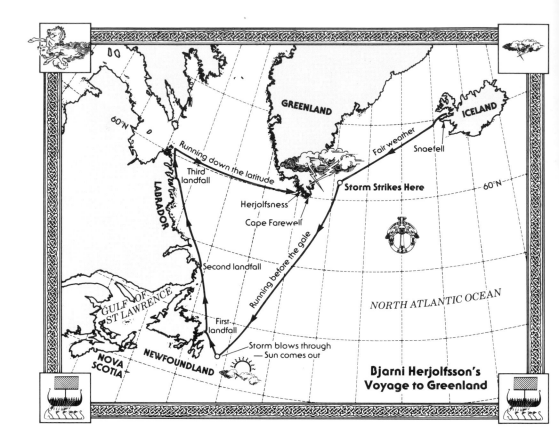

Bjarni Herjolfsson's Voyage to Greenland

also run up many miles in, quite possibly, the wrong direction but this could not be helped. It is by no means unusual for a boat of this size to make 5 knots downwind in a strong gale with no sails set. That means Bjarni was probably making between a hundred and a hundred-and-fifty miles a day.

The storm lasted for 'many days'. Because of the fog, the sailors would have had no idea in the end what the wind direction was, and hence into which *airt* they were headed. In fact, winds of this nature that endure for such a time in the vicinity of Greenland and the Labrador Sea generally blow from the north-east. Bjarni, therefore, probably went scudding away to the south and west.

Like all gales the north-easter finally blew itself out and the sun reappeared. It was immediately obvious to Bjarni that he was way to the southward of Cape Farewell.

Because the concept of even relative longitude was still centuries in the future, his chances of finding Cape Farewell by a straight shot were negligible. He had neither cross-coordinates for his present position, nor for where he was going. For a safe arrival his ship had to be placed on the same latitude as Cape Farewell but that in itself was not enough. When he reached that line he had to know whether the Cape lay to the eastward or the westward of his position. If he could be sure of which, then in order to arrive at his destination he had only to run down his latitude in the right direction until he got there. Starting as he was from an unknown point well to the south, a course into either the northeast or northwest *airt* would place him sufficiently to one side or other of the Cape for him to be confident of which way to turn when he reached the desired latitude.

His reasoning now was quite simple. 'If I sail north-east I may end up back in Europe, which would be grim for morale. Also I will then have to work westwards against the westerly winds and the current. If, on the other hand, I trend north-west, the sea may well be empty of land – certainly none has been found so far – but if I find any at all it must lie to the westward of the south Greenland Cape because there is no land between the Cape and Ireland. If that happens I will only have to work north until I find the right latitude and then run down it to the eastwards.' So that is what he did, and the following day Bjarni Herjolfsson became the first seaman from the Old World to officially set eyes upon the American continent.

Far away the land lay low on the western horizon. It didn't look like the description of Greenland that Bjarni had been given and, anyway, he knew the latitude was wrong, but his curiosity was naturally aroused and he sailed in for a closer look. The mysterious country was well-wooded and the coast was backed by small hills. Seeing the stands of timber must have made him sit up because Iceland and, for all he knew, Greenland as well, were notoriously short of lumber of building quality, both for ships and houses. However, with his *knarr* already deep-laden with high-value cargo, he had no room even to take on samples. Furthermore, the sailing season was growing old and he was anxious to get back to a known position, so he turned his ship's bow to the northward and bowled away from the coast before a south-west breeze.

In order to make sense of keeping to his original plan he maintained his heading on the western edge of the northern *airt* and two days later he made another landfall. The hands, ever hopeful, jostled round Bjarni the navigator, asking him if he thought they'd made it.

'No,' he replied. 'Greenland is full of snow peaks and glaciers. This surely isn't it. Also we are many *doegr* to the southwards of the right height of the Pole Star.' But once again, he noted the wonderful forests that grew green right down to the water's edge.

Shortly after closing the land the wind died and the *knarr* was left slatting and banging in the left-over swell. In spite of his desire to investigate what was clearly new ground, Bjarni had made up his mind that it was Greenland or bust for him. Any attempt to go ashore now would waste time and involve him in disciplinary problems rounding up the crew to sail onwards.

The hands, however, had other ideas. A deputation came shuffling aft to where he stood resolutely at the steering oar. 'Here's how it is, Captain,' growled the ringleaders. 'The men think we should go ashore and see what there is. We owe it to the whole community not just to ourselves.'

Bjarni repeated his decision and retreated not an inch.

'All that's as may be,' went on the spokesman, 'but we're going to need water and firewood before too long. We all say you should put in to the shore.'

But still Bjarni stood his ground. The men were outfaced and they dispersed grumbling aboard the *knarr*. Bjarni must have been wondering just how far he could push what was, in reality, a perfectly good crew who were merely reacting to an unusually frustrating voyage when, in the nick of time, the sea gods came to his rescue.

A fresh breeze sprang up out of the south-west. As it came on the spirits of the sailors rose with it as they always have done and always will do. Soon the confrontation was left astern as the ship sailed away to the north-north-west and out of sight of land once more.

They ran northward for three *doegr* while the Pole Star rose steadily towards the critical mark on Bjarni's star stick. When it was nearly at the same altitude as at Bergen in Norway, they came upon what they took to be a third country. This time it was high, barren and topped with a glacier and the hopes of all hands must have soared. However, Bjarni must by now have been confident that he was substantially to the west of his destination and, after a while, he announced that this land was totally worthless.

What his long-suffering crew made of that statement is left unreported by the saga tellers, but just at the strategic moment when the skipper knew he had found his latitude and knew beyond a shadow of doubt that he must now turn eastwards, the coast fizzled out and he saw that the land he had been skirting was in fact an island, or at least nothing remotely the size of Greenland.

Any suggestion from the more unenlightened deckhands that they had been cruising northward along the east side of Greenland was thus put to ridicule and, with success assured, Bjarni set his

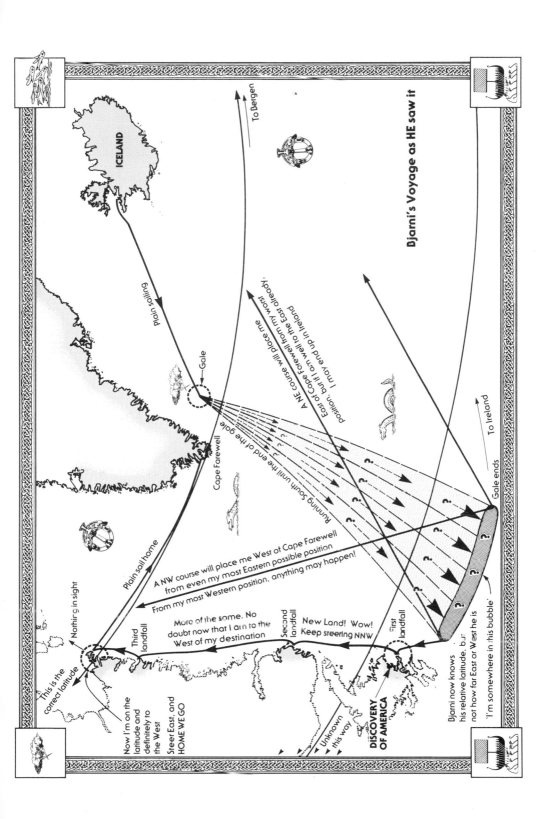

The weather map for the day Hirta left Iceland bound for Cape Farewell. Note the slack isobars west of Iceland and also the classic frontal depression flexing its muscles over Nova Scotia. This arrived in Hirta's vicinity two days later bringing strong gales

course due east and blasted off out to sea before a rising gale. Before long it was blowing old boots and the *knarr* was hard pressed to carry her canvas, but her able crew kept her driving, and driving in the right direction this time, so that four days after leaving their final discovery astern, they came upon the imposing snow peaks that back the islands and fjords of Cape Farewell.

There, lying on a promontory was a small craft that Bjarni recognised to his great relief as Herjolf's and, to a hero's welcome, he brought his ship around what was now called Herjolfness and anchored in front of his father's new home.

Bjarni's voyage is one of the greatest pieces of deductive navigation of all time, but in addition to his brilliant seamanship, he held his crew together to the end and delivered his cargo in one piece. He had fulfilled the purpose of his voyage and no sailor can do more than that, but during the long winter nights that followed, many of the Greenlanders began muttering among themselves. It was a poor sort of Norseman, they grizzled, who failed to deliver a full report on such exciting new discoveries.

They were quick enough to criticise Bjarni, but it took them years before they would put their own lives on the line in order to go and find out for themselves.

R ATHER than enjoying a passage-making breeze such as Bjarni had on his first few days out of Iceland, *Hirta*, true to the weathermen's predictions, had no wind at all. We had decided after much debate that the most sensible plan would be to sail down as best we could towards Cape Farewell and see what things were like when we got there. It was now the last week in July and, with any luck at all, the wind would change on the way and shift the ice before we arrived. The distance to run was about six hundred miles so we could well be into the beginning of August before we were close enough for the pack to become a problem. By then, time would be running short, so we would either dive quickly into Eiriksfjord if conditions permitted, or sail on towards Newfoundland in the wake of Bjarni if they did not.

Hirta's radio communication equipment is limited to a short-range VHF transmitter. This excellent device enables her to talk to shore stations when

(overleaf) The morning watch tidies up the foredeck after a nasty night; note well-reefed mainsail in close-hauled state and dinghy full of unseamanlike junk in foreground

she is within about twenty-five miles of the coast, and at sea with passing ships, but once she sets out on passage the silence of the ocean descends upon her. In general terms this is not a bad thing because the total lack of any outside information helps to encourage a seamanlike appreciation of what is going on around us. When a boat of *Hirta*'s performance is committed to a course of action, a weather forecast, for example, would not be much help. This is because her speed is not great enough to take tactical advantage of what the Met Office is offering. If there is going to be a gale, the signs are there in the sea and sky anyway, and there is little we can do about it. It seems preferable to hone one's senses to read the natural indications of what is about to happen than to spend inordinate amounts of money so that someone you don't know can invade your world twice a day and tell you. Weather reports are an invaluable assistance in coastal sailing where commitment is a day-to-day thing. On the ocean, what will come will come, and it is a question of personal choice whether you want to be advised about it or not.

On this occasion, however, a powerful radio set would have worked its passage – not because of its ability to receive weather forecasts, but by virtue of the fact that we could have tuned in to the regular international ice reports. These would have given detailed information that we could well have done with. However, as we said to ourselves daily, ships had sailed around south Greenland for hundreds of years before radios and official ice reports were heard of.

'And look what happened to them!' remarked John who was reading about Sir John Franklin's lost expedition. We didn't discuss the question any more after that.

The waters to the south-west of Iceland proved to be a riot of sealife of all kinds. Motoring through the lifeless air we spied what appeared to be a forty-five-gallon oil drum floating in our track. Mike eased the helm a spoke or two and *Hirta* cruised by the object. As we came alongside we could see that it obviously wasn't an oil drum at all. It was the dorsal fin of an enormous basking shark.

'Why isn't it sticking up in the air like a real shark's fin?' enquired Mike who was closer than some of us to schoolboy comics full of pirates, palm trees and 'sinister triangular fins cutting the water'.

'Because the beast is bone idle,' replied John, always a mine of information on natural history. 'Those creatures stuff krill down themselves just like the baleen whales. They cruise around with their mouths open and it all happens for them. No effort is required, so they have no enthusiasm for life, you see? They're too big to be bothered by predators. That one is all of twenty feet long. His liver alone probably weighs over a ton!'

'I think if I had it easy like that, I'd swim down to the Tropics, then my days would be perfect,' said Mike dreamily.

'No krill in the Tropics,' was John's bald reply but before they could continue with this unprofitable conversation the ocean all around us erupted with a million porpoises. From horizon to horizon they swam, plunged and leapt twirling into the air. Hannah and Ros came rushing up on deck and for a whole hour we all watched spellbound. Then quite suddenly, they were gone.

'Where do they go to?' Hannah wanted to know; but no-one can say how it is that in a matter of seconds a whole nation of air-breathing sea mammals can disappear entirely from the view of a waterborne observer.

'I've never seen a display like that before,' whistled Patrick.

'You know what they say, don't you?' began John. Predictably, no-one did. '"When the sea hog jumps, look to your pumps!"'

'That's a load of rubbish,' sneered Chris, more in hope than conviction. 'The glass is steady, the sky's clear and they're enjoying the day as much as us; besides, the weathermen said there'd be nothing nasty for several days yet.'

John said no more but by three o'clock the following morning *Hirta* was hove-to with the jib rolled in, the staysail shortened down and the mainsail close-reefed in a heavy gale out of the south-east.

After a couple of hours the wind was down to Force 8 and the barometer, which had just dropped nine points in under four hours, was steadying off. The sea was building with the wind and a greasy grey fog was swirling around us. Now that it was blowing only a moderate gale we let draw the staysail and *Hirta* began shouldering her way towards Cape Farewell.

Patrick and Ros were relighting the cabin stove. It was sorely needed to dry out the accommodation because in the early stages of the blow an awkward wave had broken clean over the boat, penetrated the skylight and washed out the saloon. Pat was grunting with exertion as he wrestled another bag of coal out from under the cockpit. There was half-a-ton of it down there, 'and a good thing too,' said Chris from the helm, 'but the sooner he starts feeding it up the chimney and into the atmosphere the better.'

Chris, Mike and I were huddled in the cockpit and for a while we said nothing as the daylight grew stronger and the smoke began to pour out of the 'charley noble' to be whipped away to leeward by the downdraught from the mainsail.

It was Chris who broke our silence. 'I've been thinking for the past half hour about this Bjarni Herjolfsson guy,' he said, 'and I don't see how you can be so sure that he made his first landfall in Newfoundland. I mean, the saga doesn't say how long his northerly gale lasted. It doesn't even specify that it stayed in the north at all. He might have ended up in Nova Scotia. I've even heard people say that he touched on Cape Cod.'

'I was wondering that too,' added Mike, 'but I'm not sure myself that it really matters. Surely the main thing is that he must have sighted some place in North America?'

161

'In the end, I think that's the most sensible approach,' I agreed. 'It's not going to change the sovereignty of the USA or Canada either way, but we wouldn't be normal if we weren't curious.'

'So what's your reasoning?' said Chris, determined to ferret out whether we were sailing on a hunch or a rationale. As he spoke a heavy sea broke under the stern and we were all hammered by the spray which flew across the cockpit. *Hirta* lifted her skirts daintily and surged on into the dawn.

'Here's how I reckon it,' I explained, as I took another turn around my neck with the ten-foot-long red scarf Ros had knitted while tending the bar in a Salisbury pub. 'You're quite right, we aren't told how far Bjarni was driven to the south, and all the distances and directions in the saga are vague by our standards. But never forget that he had no idea of the existence of any land at all down there. He had no charts and no longitude. He didn't even know his latitude in the same way we do. It was just a comparative measurement of the height of Polaris from various known locations.'

'Then why are you so sure?'

'Because I know that above all else that man was a seaman and a navigator, not an ordinary Viking who did a bit of sailing between rape-and-plunder appointments. Wherever else he went, one place is absolutely certain. The saga says that on the final leg of his passage he left the land and sailed for four days and then fetched up at Cape Farewell. The only possible way he could have done that would have been to know before he took his departure that he was on the correct latitude. There is only one place four days run from Cape Farewell anywhere near the same latitude and that is Cape Chidley at the tip of northern Labrador. The saga also says that the coast ended there. The teller says that they thought the land was an island, but the main point is that there was no more land visible to the north.'

'Perhaps he just had a feeling about where he was and took a flyer for Cape Farewell from somewhere different.' Chris suggested.

'Not a hope, mate,' I replied. 'That guy was a professional. Because he didn't know anything about longitude, and had no chart either, he couldn't work a traverse to Cape Farewell from anywhere in North America at that time, even if he got lucky.'

'Why not?'

'Because he had no coordinates for where he was. The only chance he had was to run his latitude. And that is what he did. If you now work backwards in days' runs . . .'

'What's a day's run again for a *knarr*?'

'About the same as us, 120 to 150 miles on a good day . . . If you work backwards you find that his last landfall, the one with the glacier, was northern Labrador and the Torngat Mountains. The second was southern Labrador, perhaps in the Lake Melville area, and the initial touch must have been eastern Newfoundland. The topography checks out as well.'

Mike nodded thoughtfully inside his oilskin hood. 'It was a bit of luck for him that he came across the land so soon after the storm wasn't it?' he said.

It was Chris who replied. 'Everyone needs a break now and again. We could do with one ourselves. You draw the water, skipper, and I'll pump her out again.'

I carefully dunked the bucket over the side on its lanyard and, as always, it tried hard to jerk me into the Greenland Sea.

I poured the icy water down the pump barrel to prime the device and Chris worked the handle steadily. After two hundred strokes the bilge was clear and I went below to a warm dry saloon.

All that day the wind blew hard as the so-called warm sector between the fronts of the depression roared past en route for Iceland and points north. By midnight the cold front was upon us with a sharply rising barometer, storm-force winds and a vicious cross-sea.

All hands turned out into the freezing twilight. The storm was howling down straight out of the west now, directly from the two-mile-thick ice cap of Greenland. *Hirta* was hove-to with only two reefs in the mainsail. Each time the canvas kicked the mast looked ready to jump out of the deck. The air was so heavy with cold that it hurt to turn and face the wind. It wasn't a *hafgerdingar*, but we had definitely lost that feeling of security we had talked about between the Faeroe Islands and Iceland. Cape Farewell seemed an insurmountable distance away.

Easy for Leif the Lucky, a hard grind for Hirta

NOT everyone who tried to traverse the Greenland Sea received the sort of hiding dished up to Bjarni Herjolfsson. *Hirta* looked as if she was going to take a hammering a thousand years later and eleven out of the original twenty-five Greenland emigrant ships failed to arrive, but for some the passage went smoothly enough. Ten years after its inception, Eirik's colony was thriving and a regular trade route to Iceland – and even direct to Norway – had been established.

Eirik's dream had solidified into reality. Now in his middle forties his power was established, his wealth was steadily growing and all the inhabitants of the Greenland fjords recognised him as supreme chief. As he had predicted, the fur and ivory products for which the country was becoming well-known were forming the basis of a sound economy, and more land-hungry Icelanders were settling there each spring.

Just as in Iceland, there was a serious grain shortage and, in consequence, bread and beer were scarce, but as the years went by an even more desperate deficiency began to make itself felt. Timber was almost non-existent. The lack of this vital commodity was common throughout the Norse western ocean communities from the Faeroes outwards, but in Greenland it soon became acute. Although its value was grossly inflated, wood didn't make an attractive cargo for merchants from Europe on account of its bulk. Silks, wines, iron tools, weapons and other high-cost, low-volume wares were still a more profitable proposition. By 995 the situation was getting out of hand.

During this period, Eirik the Red's family had been growing up. He had three sons, the eldest of whom was Leif.

In his twenty-five years Leif Eiriksson had seen plenty of action. His earliest memories would include fireside tales of Eirik's deeds of death and glory in the fields of Haukadale. As a child he had lain awake at night with his heart in his throat wondering if his father would come home again from the bloody meetings with Eyjolf the Foul and Holm-gang Hrafn. While still a boy he had watched Eirik depart for the unknown western wilderness, and as a youth he had greeted his return. The homesteading, the land clearing, the cries of the whale hunts and the deadly stalking of the walrus on the ice were all a part of his life. By the age of eighteen he would have been a trained and able warrior. Now, in his prime, he was suffering agonies of frustration.

A tall, strong figure, he was well enough liked and there was no shortage of men ready to follow his lead. Leif's whole background and education fitted him for the doing of heroic deeds and the acquisition of wealth and fame in his own right, but his geographical situation was against him. He was the son of the chief in an outpost at the end of the known world; the raiding life of a young Viking was denied him, ordinary trading he would consider beneath his dignity, and he was in all probability rather afraid of going to Norway to seek his fortune lest more sophisticated bandits of the King's court treat him as a bumpkin from the provinces. But deep inside Leif Eiriksson there glowed a spark of the flame that had powered his father's pioneering successes. Reasoning to himself that house- and ship-building were almost at a standstill, he recalled the tale told over the fire by Bjarni years before concerning forested land far away to the south-west. Anyone who sailed into Greenland with a shipload of hardwood must surely boost his prestige, to say nothing of the opportunity for quick money so beloved by all Norsemen. He, Leif, had plenty of followers to crew a ship, but unfortunately he hadn't got a vessel.

Once his mind was made up, however, a small problem like this wasn't going to stand in his way and he journeyed down to Herjolfness to visit Bjarni.

Bjarni was the same age as Leif's father and after his great voyage he had laid up his *knarr* and swallowed the anchor. We don't know whether he took much persuading but in the end he sold his ship to Leif and gave him what instructions he could for finding the forested lands. For a navigator of Bjarni's class it wouldn't have been difficult to give Leif a course to steer direct to the land he had first sighted. Bjarni would surely have noted the latitude of his discovery; he knew that his course from there to the point he finally turned east to run down to Greenland had been along the western edge of the northern *airt*, and he knew how many *doegr* he had run to the eastwards to Herjolfsness. Thus he had two sides of the triangle. The third was the course and distance direct.

The various saga accounts of Leif's voyages are at loggerheads on so many points that in the end the student can only make up his own mind on the question of the route he took to the south and west. However from what we know of Leif's character and motivations it seems most likely that after victualling ship he set an undeviating course for the far horizon with his eyes full of dollar signs.

Unlike the experiences of most of us who have sailed these waters, Leif's trip was a piece of cake. He climbed on to a solid north-east wind and zoomed straight down to what he assumed was Bjarni's land. Whether it was or not is irrelevant. What is important is that when Leif and his men stepped ashore they found a world of plenty beyond their wildest northern dreams.

The rivers were jammed with the largest salmon ever; the pastureland was lush enough to feed all the cattle in Norway; wheat grew abundantly in the wild state, so only Odin knew what could be produced by a careful farmer, and the endless virgin forests contained more hardwood than you needed to build a hundred fleets.

One day after the men had been exploring, an old German retainer of Eirik's came rambling back behind the others. This worthy had an odd face at the best of times with a dome-like forehead and a shifty appearance, but on this occasion he looked even worse than usual. His eyes were rolling and he was gibbering something in German that none of the Norsemen could understand. Finally he came out of his fit and announced that he had found wild vines full of grapes just down the way. This seemed too much to hope for. Since neither Leif nor any of his men knew what a grapevine looked like they were tempted to ridicule the old boy but he soon stopped their laughter when he told them that he'd grown up surrounded by vines in the wine-growing valleys of Germany. Then they knew they'd struck gold.

Timber was one thing. It was a valuable asset and the importance of this place would undoubtedly be based upon it but Leif was as canny as his father. He knew people needed a dream. For a Viking living out his life in the sunless valleys of the sub-Arctic communities, the promise of the warmth of summer locked in the skin of a wine berry would be a truly exotic image.

That night over their evening meal Leif told his crew what was in his mind. 'Here's what we'll do, lads,' he announced with his mouth full of barbecued moose. 'When we fill the ship with wood, we'll

(opposite) After over seventy years Hirta's spars show
signs of yet more hard work

166

load a pile of the grapes as well. We'll call this country Vinland after the wine berries and, before you know it, the place will become a legend.'

Leif and his gang spent an easy winter in Vinland and the following spring they sailed for Greenland. The *knarr* that had done so well by Bjarni stomped home in grand style and, after what seems to have been another cushy passage, the familiar ice mountains rose above the horizon to greet them. It was clear early on that with the wind that was blowing they could lay their course to Eiriksfjord on a comfortable reach but, after a while, one of the hands noticed that Leif, who was steering, was sailing well 'above' the course.

'What are you up to, pointing so high on the wind?' he enquired naturally enough.

'I'm watching my heading, don't worry!' snapped Leif; then he decided to explain himself. 'See that reef up on the weather bow? I'm not sure, but I think it has a wrecked ship on it, with people waving.'

No-one else aboard could make it out but Leif, who of course is billed as a superstar, had the best eyes on board. Sure enough, he was proved right and, in due course, they anchored to leeward of the reef. After making sure that the folk stranded upon it were *bona fide* shipwrecked sailors and not pirates doing the old 'mariners in distress' routine, he struck a bargain.

Their lives in exchange for their goods . . .

This unexpected booty worked marvels for the profits of Leif's expedition. These had been good to begin with but now they were extraordinary and the *knarr*, awash with riches, rolled crankily into the home fjord while his men chanted his name.

It's true to say that a sailor makes his own luck. On this voyage Leif was given all the breaks he needed but he handled his crew effectively and made the most of every chance so his fortune was well merited. Shortly after his return someone coined the nickname Leif the Lucky. It stuck for the rest of his life.

That winter was a bad one in Greenland. The survivors from the reef brought plague with them from Norway and many good men and women died in the dimly-lit turf halls during the long frozen night. Eirik's family survived intact, however, and as the cattle were driven back out into the meadows to meet the approaching springtime, Leif agreed to loan his *knarr* to his brother, Thorvald, who was determined to make his own Vinland voyage, and keep the profits rolling in.

But it seemed that all Eirik's luck had rubbed off onto Leif. His younger sons found themselves wrestling with a very different fate.

WHEN Messrs Slade and Sons of Fowey installed the pitch pine mast into Pilot Morrice's new cutter in 1911, they did not expect that either spar or vessel would still be around seventy-five years later. Ever since I have owned *Hirta* people who think they know better than those elder statesmen have been offering me unsolicited opinions on their work. 'Don't you think the mast's a bit thin?' they enquire, casting a knowing eye on its mere 8½in width.

The only reply to these critics is: 'No. Do you?' This puts them on the spot and I can go on to explain that the old stick has stood well enough for threequarters of a century. If one then considers that this is almost a tenth of the total elapsed time since Leif and his lads brought home the bacon, it places an interesting perspective on all sorts of things.

The spar is a grown tree shaped by adze and plane rather than a sophisticated glued-up hollow job. All the natural strength and suppleness are retained and if you watch its antics as the boat sails hard in a rough sea you realise that it conforms perfectly to the old rigger's maxim, 'If it don't bend, it'll break'.

Hirta's mast writhes and twists like a live thing. In spite of this, John and I were looking at it pretty hard as the boat lay hove-to in the half-light of the midnight gale.

'Do you think it can stand?' I asked. 'She's got far more canvas than she can carry.' This blow had come on so quickly that we'd had no time to pull down the deep reef.

'Why don't we put the reef in now?' Chris wanted to know.

Patrick, the strongest man on board, said it before John or I could reply. 'Not a chance, mate,' he grunted. 'You'd probably get a rupture heaving down the clew cringle, and even if you survived that, there's no way we'd tie the points. It's too late.'

'So, we've got two choices,' I summed up. 'Either the sail stays where it is, or it comes down altogether.'

For several minutes no-one said another word. We were all thinking the same thing: dropping that amount of canvas in this wind and sea wasn't going to be just unpleasant, it was going to be downright dangerous. There was enough power in it to drive 30 tons of boat at 10 knots right now. As soon as the halyards were let off and it began spilling wind, the thing would go berserk.

As we lurked indecisively round the wheel *Hirta* fell off a giant breaking sea and the sail gave a single thunderous clap. Ros appeared in the companionway and took a brief look at the scenery.

'I dunno what you're all sitting around for,' she said. 'It's got to go, hasn't it?'

We knew she was right. If we didn't drop the sail there and then, it might drop itself any minute, and take the mast with it over the side.

169

Mike and John crawled forward. They set up the weather topping lift, and flaked the halyards so they would run without a snag. Patrick waited in the cockpit and Chris stood by festooned with heavy sail ties which were flying and whipping like paper streamers around his neck. I had volunteered to secure the gaff-end, which promised to be a memorable struggle. Either I got a round turn on it in short order, or it would lift me over the rail like a rag doll. The water temperature was 2°C, so that would mark the end of my problems.

Poised to fight the good fight we waited for a 'smooth' in the sea. Because the boat was hove-to the helm was lashed in such a way that she was trying to turn into the wind. She could not do so, however, because the staysail was sheeted hard to weather and holding her bow down. This arrangement results in the boat finding an equilibrium about 40° from the wind. In order to drop the mainsail in these conditions we needed to come briefly head to wind and the simplest way to achieve this was to ease the staysail across to leeward. *Hirta* would then round up of her own accord, falling off once more as she stalled, by which time the main would be on the deck. We hoped.

On the word, Ros surged the tail of the windward staysail sheet around its cleat and Patrick sweated in the one on the lee side like a madman. It was done in a matter of seconds and straightaway *Hirta* began to luff into the wind. I waited until the mainsail emptied itself of air and began flogging and then called to John and Mike.

'Bring her down, boys!'

The sail came in with an ease that astonished us all and I found myself looking bemused at the end of the gaff which was lying obediently on top of the boom waiting for me to put a tie round it. I couldn't believe my luck and for far too long I stared at the 28ft spar that should by rights have been trying to hurl us all into the sea; then I grabbed it and in no time the worst danger was over.

Subduing the canvas took the six of us over half an hour. The cold and associated wind chill was so intense that our fingers were numb after five minutes. The sailcloth was stiff with ice and seemed as inflexible as a barn door so that every contact resulted in some minor wound or other which we did not feel till later. Just when the job looked beaten a wave broke over the rail and washed us all into the lee scuppers where the pitiless sea soaked us to the bone. The sail broke loose, and we started all over again. By virtue of the perfection of her hull form *Hirta* lay quietly throughout the struggle with her helm lashed. Even without the mainsail to keep her head up, her deep forefoot held the bow higher than beam-on to the waves and she made no serious attempt to throw us over the side.

When we'd finished the job it was one o'clock and Ros thoughtfully served up a jug of coffee that was more than half whisky. As the hail squalls fresh from the pack ice drove across the deck Chris lounged in the bottom of the

Ros takes a trick at the wheel in the sub-Arctic twilight

cockpit wearing a lop-sided smirk.

'I never knew before that I had the second sight,' he sipped the last of his firewater and hiccupped, 'but when we were all standing about like lemons waiting for the skipper to take a turn around the gaff I'd swear I saw a little old man wearing a pilot's cap hanging onto it for him.'

'He was probably persuading him to stop scratching his bum and give the rest of us a hand to save ourselves,' suggested Mike.

As for me I said nothing because at the crucial moment of the sail stowing I too had experienced the distinct impression that we were not by ourselves. Once or twice in a crisis at sea I have had the same feeling and just now the gaff had sat there waiting for me in defiance of all the laws of nature; but then, as Leif Eiriksson had discovered, everybody needs a stroke of luck now and again.

After this session the wind blew hard from exactly where we wanted to go for a whole day. For the first twelve hours there was no question of sailing. Like Bjarni, we were concerned simply with surviving the storm, although because of the differences in our boats and the wind direction our tactics and

171

his were totally at variance. By the afternoon the breeze was down to Force 7 but still squarely on the nose, so we elected to remain hove-to and lick our wounds. We did go so far as to re-hoist the mainsail which was now quite docile with its two reefs still in.

Shortly after midnight, twenty-four hours on from Pilot Morrice's spectral visit, we let draw the staysail and began beating to the south-west. At first we could point no closer than 50° to the desired heading but we were grateful to be underway at all.

'It's going to be a long way if we don't get a better deal than this,' said John, which was the truth. 'Do you suppose that was the depression on its way from Nova Scotia that Thor Jakobsson promised us?' he continued. 'Because if it was, it must have wound itself up far more than anyone expected.'

'It must have been,' I replied, glancing at the sky to the westward, 'and I think the next one is going to be with us shortly. With luck though, we'll be able to tack on the wind shifts at the fronts if they aren't too violent, and make a reasonable amount of ground as each one goes through. The barometer's falling now and it looks as though the wind is backing more into the south.'

It was, and by breakfast time we were making 4½ knots through a wicked sea with Cape Farewell almost ahead though still four hundred miles away. We were now four days out, and had made good hardly more than one third of the distance.

Cape Farewell,
Ivan and the commissar

THE one thing in *Hirta*'s favour as she struggled, thrashed and staggered her way uphill towards Cape Farewell was that, as yet, she was in no danger from drifting ice. According to the pilot chart issued by the United States Defense Mapping Agency, winds in general between Iceland and Greenland in August favour the northern quadrant. The specific average wind reports covering our particular track suggested that we had better than even chances of a breeze from the quarter we wanted. Ice did not appear on the bill of fare until we began to close the Cape itself.

Unfortunately, while the predictions turned out to be correct in the ice department, the wind blew sternly in our teeth day after day. The depressions whistled by just to the northward of our track giving us a variety of gale- and near gale-force weather, but wherever the wind blew from there was always more west in it than we could handle. In spite of this wretched and unpromised state of affairs, however, things could have been worse. In the human comfort sector the situation was as bad as it was likely to get, short of actual drowning, but the fact that the wind does shift frequently under the influence of fast-moving low-pressure circulations allowed us to make at least spasmodic progress towards the south-west.

When we were about halfway a couple of depressions slipped to the southward of the railway lines on which the others seemed to be running and their centres passed right over us. These systems generated conditions of abject misery because as the round part without isobars that has 'low' written across it on the weather maps trundled by there would be a period of anything up to twelve hours with no wind at all. The sea then came at us from all directions and the ship's gear was subject to intolerable strains. So were the nerves of the crew. These calms often brought thick fog and freezing cold, while the noise of the gear crashing about on deck made certain that no-one got any sleep.

The chief culprit of the noise-making was the main boom and, in

173

particular, the mainsheet blocks. One of these hangs under the boom itself while the other three are sited on the aft deck. They weigh up to twenty pounds. When the boom snatches in light airs and a choppy sea they jerk upright and then bang down on the deck with a fearful racket. The central lower sheet block on its own sounds like the percussion section of a nightmare symphony orchestra. It is attached to the counter by way of a system of meaty springs and stirrups designed to absorb just such shock loads. While the arrangement is kind to the structure of *Hirta*'s stern overhang, it is downright brutal to the watch below.

All manner of devices were contrived to stop this bedlam but in the end the only one which worked was to pull the mainsheet hard amidships and take up all the slack. This had the side-effect of stopping the boat dead in the water which was even worse for morale.

Finally we resorted to the engine. Fuel was in limited supply, but as Chris put it so succinctly, 'We may as well motor out of this and find ourselves another gale. At least then we'll be able to catch up on some sleep.'

He wasn't disappointed. We motored under the centre of the low as it moved through in the opposite directions, and soon we were rewarded with a moderate gale out of the west-north-west. By taking this on the starboard tack we could make a course only 70° or so away from where we wanted to go. When the wind backed into the south on the approach of the next front we went about and were almost able to lay our course on the port tack. And so on.

It took *Hirta* eleven days to reach the southern tip of Greenland in this unrelenting foul weather. By the time she arrived the only dry place left was Hannah's cabin. This little haven of joy is opposite the galley and since it is right on the ship's pitching pivot point it is also the part of the accommodation that is least subject to the motion of the sea. Ros shared the cabin with Hannah for this section of the voyage but since she spent most of the daytime planning, cooking or clearing up after meals her berth was in high demand by the watch below. Not even the happy 'child at play with assorted soggy stuffed animal' noises could deter the daytime dossers.

The forecabin where Ros and I can usually cling onto whatever privacy is possible in a 50ft pilot cutter was a total washout. No-one went in there any more. So many seas had come rushing two feet deep across the foredeck that

(opposite) Chris models his Cape Farewell helmsman's outfit: cap ex-Faeroe Islands gutter, jacket ex-Swedish army ex-unknown sheep, gloves knitted by Oxfam lady, trousers ex-Transworld Expedition sell-off sale, wellies ex-Sussex Farmers Co-op. Total cost £9.50. Satisfaction total

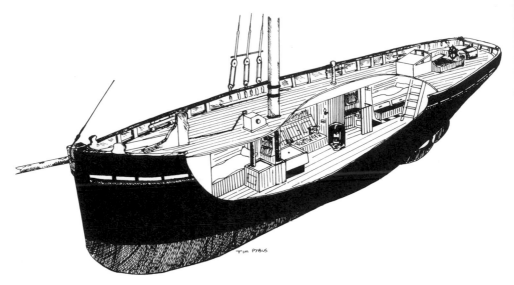

Cutaway section showing Hirta's *accommodation*

the forehatch over the bunk had given up the struggle to maintain its watertight integrity. We shut the door in despair on this chamber of horrors and anything left up there had to take its chance.

Hot-bunking on the two saloon settees and the quarter-berth were the only possibilities that remained once Ros had gone to bed. The benefit of the saloon was that the fire pumped its heat out regardless of what the icy sea threw at us. This meant that although the skylight and the coamings leaked to an extent that even an amphibian would have found unacceptable, at least the incumbents were warm as well as wet through. The fire also dried the cabin out quickly whenever the state of affairs in the world outside calmed down sufficiently to allow the deck to empty itself of water.

The quarter-berth is situated just inside the companionway opposite the engine. Officially this was Chris' private stronghold but he generously sublet it while he was on watch to anyone who could no longer face the steamy delights of the saloon and who had enough moral fibre to cope with his dead-sheep coat. The quarter-berth offers a much drier bed than one might suppose, but it too is subject to unexpected sources of insomnia. The pump is hard by the beneficiary's left ear and it is a man of iron who can lie there and ignore the temptation to count the strokes of the hourly session called for by the heavy weather. Thirty strokes and things are going well; that is 'SLR' – Standard Leak Rate for moderate windward sailing. A hundred strokes is about par in a heavy beat in a steep sea, a hundred-and-fifty and you are beginning to wonder. Over two hundred and the sleeper is on record as

176

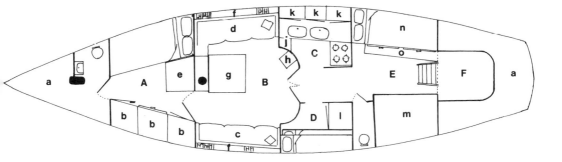

Plan of Hirta's *accommodation*

A	*forecabin*	e *chain locker*
B	*saloon*	f *bookshelves*
C	*galley*	g *table*
D	*Hannah's cabin*	h *heating stove*
E	*companionway*	j *airing cupboard*
F	*cockpit*	k *lockers*
a	*stowage*	l *hanging locker*
b	*wardrobe/dressing table*	m *chart table (engine room beneath)*
c	*settee*	n *quarterberth*
d	*settee/berth*	o *toolbox*

having been seen appearing in the companionway, a sepulchral figure in a pyjama top clutching a tattered life jacket.

If he has the *sangfroid* to ignore the sucking and wheezing of the pump he still has to shut his ears to the happy murmurs of cockpit gossip filtering down through the companionway doors:

'My oilies leak.'

'Not half so much as *Hirta*'s garboards!'

'Do you think she's spewed some of her caulking?'

'Nah. It'll take up as soon as the wind frees and she stops hammering into this head sea.'

A short pause is brought to an end by the thump of a wave breaking under the turn of the bilge and the sputtering sound of spray on inadequate waterproofs.

'---t!'

'Why don't you watch where you're steering?'

'Never mind that, it's two o'clock. Better give her another pump.'

One . . . Two . . . Three . . .

Hirta's topsail stayed rolled firmly around its 15ft yard for the whole of this passage. Both items stow in a long sailcloth bag like a huge sausage skin known, inevitably, as The Condom. This is hung on the rail. The only thought we gave it for two weeks was a passing concern lest it should be washed away. The real tragedy of the trip was that seven days out, again in a period of no wind and a terrible sea, we had carried away the luffwire of the spitfire jib. This tiny sail makes all the difference to the boat's performance on the wind in bad weather. Most of the breeze we were receiving was far too fierce for the big jib. Penury had ruled that the working jib so comprehensively destroyed on day one of the voyage off Brighton Marina was going to stay for the time being on the replacement list, and so the spitfire had been more than working its passage. The nature of its injury was such that we could do nothing for it at sea and so *Hirta* was left with number one jib or nothing, which seriously damaged her performance potential.

When we were almost within sight of the last charted position of the ice edge off Cape Farewell, six hundred miles from Reykjavik, we had seen no ships. Consequently we had received no up-to-date ice information. It seemed we would just have to go and take a look, but time was now extremely short and we realised that all the westerly winds would certainly not have dispersed the pack ice blocking the coast by Eiriksfjord.

For once the wind was east of south and *Hirta* was making good progress. I was lying in the quarter berth alternately dozing and considering the technical situation when John's voice broke the peace of the afternoon watch.

'Ship in sight. No; two ships!'

I was rolling out of the bunk as he came down for the binoculars. This was just what we needed.

'What are they John, fishing boats?'

'More like factory ships, I would say. They're a way off but they're coming in our direction.'

I joined in the general crush to climb the steps. Even Hannah turned out for a peep. Up on deck it was a comparatively pleasant afternoon, certainly the best since Iceland. A big sea was still running but with the wind down to Force 4 *Hirta* was moving sedately under a high, grey sky. There, dead to leeward of us, a couple of ships were steaming steadily in line abreast, coming up on us from the direction of the pack ice. John was focussing the binoculars on one of them. At two miles range he was able to isolate some details.

'They've got fishing numbers, but I can't make them out,' he said slowly. 'If they'd turn beam on it would be easier. Ah, that's better,' he nodded as the two ships obliged him. 'Oh,' he exclaimed. 'They're Ruskies. Whopping stern trawlers; bristling with aerials. Is our set on?'

Patrick had already switched to channel 16, the international calling up

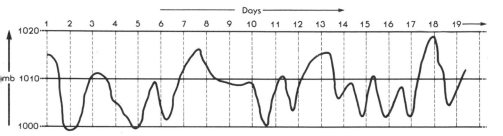

A graph of Hirta's *barometer readings between Iceland and Newfoundland.*
Although the actual range of movement is not enormous, the constantly
changing pressure and the sharpness of the peaks and troughs
indicate the severity of the weather

and distress frequency, but so far the radio was silent.

'There's probably someone on them who speaks better English than we do,' he speculated. 'They don't need aerials like those for finding fish. Let's give them a shout.'

'Right-ho!'

Patrick picked up the handset.

'Russian fishing vessel, Russian fishing vessel, this is the sailing vessel *Hirta*, sailing vessel *Hirta*, over.'

Silence; the ships steamed on oblivious, but still shortening the distance.

Patrick waited the recommended two minutes and repeated his message. Again there was no reply. Now the ships were as close as their present course would bring them. We estimated their range at one mile, which is not far at all in an ocean that has been empty for a fortnight.

'Give them one more go, Pat.'

This time the radio crackled into life and a thickly-accented voice came through with the traditional greeting of the sea.

'Vot ship is that and vere are you bound?'

I took the handset and filled him in on the details. Then I returned the courtesy.

There was no reply, but over the radio we could hear a *sotto voce* discussion going on in Russian.

By now the ships were beginning to open the distance between us, and our prospects of an ice report were looking thinner by the minute.

'Maybe they didn't understand you the first time,' said Chris. 'You might as well try again.'

So we did, and once more there was rapid and extremely Russian conversation, this time one of the voices sounded animated.

'You'd think if they were going to have a family row they'd turn off the

179

transmitter, wouldn't you?' Ros observed from her position at the helm where she had been giving John a spell. Suddenly the speaker blared out another question in the caricature accent.

'How many mens have you?'

'Cheeky devil! What's it to him?' spluttered Patrick, but I told him just the same, and then asked him for an ice report.

He ignored this request and his next message introduced a sinister note to our cosy one way chat.

'How many vimmens are aboard your ship?'

We began to wonder now about his intentions. Maybe they were six months out of Murmansk and they'd run out of naughty magazines. Ros zipped up her oilskin. Her face took on a look that would have done credit to Queen Victoria.

'Two,' I replied shortly, and added to myself, 'and they are not amused.' Aloud I continued, 'and how about yourself?'

He evaded this question with Asiatic cunning by becoming even more personal. He now required to know the name and certificate number of our captain.

'Bloody hell!' fumed Patrick. 'That's too much. Tell him your name's Captain Kidd, and this the High Seas, not the Lubyanka!'

Patrick was right. This was madness in the extreme. All we wanted was an ice report but we were seven souls in a small, wooden ship sailing a freezing, deserted ocean. They were large steel vessels probably teeming with bodies. They held all the cards. They were also certainly privy to the information we needed, and so I politely spelled out my full name and the first number which came into my head, which was the number of my bank account. Reflecting later at my leisure, I pondered on the wisdom of this irreverence. I then enquired solicitously about the welfare of their own skipper and his family and once again put in a request for the latest ice report on Cape Farewell and south-west Greenland.

Another heated discussion at the other end of the air wave ended with the unequivocal reply. 'Ve haf no ice report. Out!' With this villainous piece of unneighbourly behaviour they swung to port and cruised off towards the high Arctic.

Leaving the watch on deck glowering after the two ships I climbed, disgusted, back into the quarter-berth. I was considering the wretched state to which Adam's race had fallen and mentally disembowelling whoever it was on the trawler, presumably the commissar, who would not allow one honest seaman to talk to another, when there was a shout from the cockpit.

(opposite) The last ice chart issued to Hirta *in Iceland. Notice the heavy ice extending to the south of Greenland and also the 8/10 pack ice in the Julianehaab (Eiriksfjord) region*

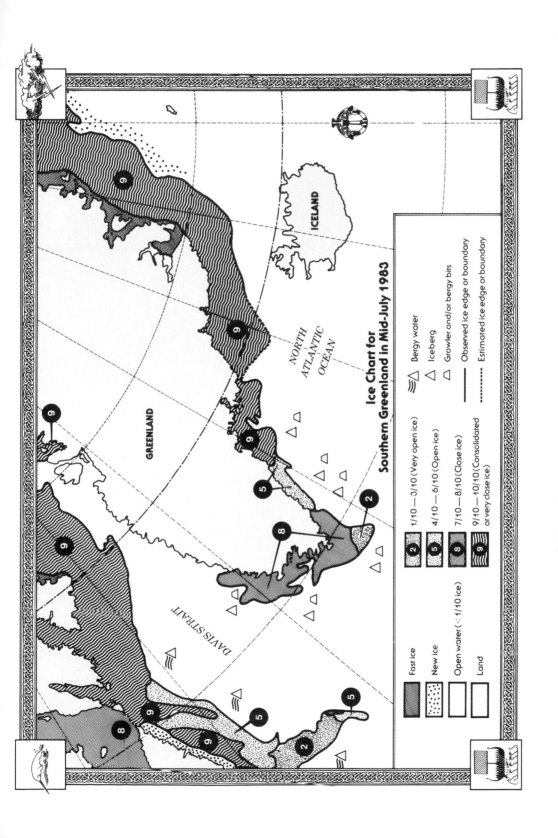

Ice Chart for
Southern Greenland in Mid-July 1983

ICELAND

GREENLAND

NORTH
ATLANTIC
OCEAN

DAVIS STRAIT

≋△ Bergy water
△ Iceberg
△ Growler and/or bergy bits
—— Observed ice edge or boundary
------ Estimated ice edge or boundary

2　1/10 — 3/10 (Very open ice)
5　4/10 — 6/10 (Open ice)
8　7/10 — 8/10 (Close ice)
9　9/10 — 10/10 (Consolidated
　　or very close ice)

Fast ice
New ice
Open water (<1/10 ice)
Land

The Russians off Cape Farewell; ladies line the foredeck,
Ivan's on the bridge wing, but where is the commissar?

'Here they come!' called Mike. 'Stand by to repel bawdies!'

I leapt up the steps and there, towering over me was the fo'c'sle head of the first trawler. The rail was lined with 4ft high women, all grinning and flapping their arms about. Their hair was tied up in dark scarves and they wore old-fashioned pinnies around their ample waists. Further aft as the ship plunged by more and more men appeared coming up from the fish rooms, all waving with a warmth that could almost be felt.

On the bridge wing, the captain was calling orders back to his mate and soon the ship was keeping station alongside us, rolling horribly in the swell. He held up a bottle in one hand and with the other he gesticulated unmistakably that we should join him.

'I think Ivan's inviting us to a party,' observed Chris laconically. 'Personally I'd rather have had an ice report.'

'He's very kind, I'm sure,' I said, as Hannah leapt up and down waving to a fat lady who was screaming something grandmotherly at her 'but I'd no more go alongside him than drive the ship up the ice. It'd be like putting her onto a cliff in an onshore gale. Look at that sea.'

No-one argued with this but the great steel wall remained resolutely where it was. The black gang came tumbling up from the engine room and one of them who had a perfectly bald head and a face like the man in the moon lobbed us a bottle of vodka. Tragically it fell far from our grasp and bobbed pitifully astern.

Patrick rushed below and reappeared almost instantly with a litre of Scotch. He raised it dramatically to his lips and then held it at arm's length towards the Russians. Afterwards he passed it round and we all did the same. Ivan got the message and as his crew all along the rail upended their own bottles he peeled off and blew his horn again and again as he steamed off for the last time.

'The commissar might be a swine,' said John, taking another quick swig, 'but we'd have had a grand night out with Ivan and the boys and girls.'

We all felt the same and so, just for luck, I tried the radio once more. My efforts were rewarded by complete and utter silence.

'So much for the politicians,' spat Ros contemptuously, her eyes watering from the neat spirit and the emotion of the occasion. 'Theirs, ours, what's the difference? Now; how far did you say you thought we were from the ice edge?'

Vinland, the stormy Atlantic and the walking dead

$\mathbf{\mathit{+}}$

THE various sagas are all in agreement on the essential facts leading up to the founding of the Greenland colony. From that point on they offer the reader a remarkable selection of chronologies and personalities.

Some of the paradoxes are readily unravelled by referring to the excellent scholastic studies on the subject. Others can be sorted out by careful reading and the application of a pinch of seamanlike common sense. A few, unfortunately, seem difficult to reconcile by either method, but this should not be taken as evidence that their overall message is erroneous. For the most part the sagas are complementary rather than mutually destructive. A character or an event left out of one will be found colourfully expressed in another. The clerics who first wrote down the sagas were working anything from fifty to a hundred-and-fifty years after the events which they were reporting. Often their manuscripts were lost or fragmented. The stories were reassembled later by writers commissioned, in most cases, by descendants of one or other of the saga heroes. These authors naturally had a political interest likely to encourage distortion in the patron's favour. The Church's influence on the content of some sagas was also considerable. Any individual with a name for Christian behaviour was likely to benefit from a good write-up, or at least a mention. Heathens were treated less generously.

No-one can lay down for sure the exact synopsis of the sundry reported voyages to and from Vinland. The sagas do not make it plain and there is not enough circumstantial evidence for anyone to be dogmatic. Fortunately, it doesn't matter any more. What did matter to *Hirta*'s crew was that these men and women had preceded us in the far-off days half a millenium before Columbus. We agreed amongst ourselves on a probable and realistic order of events. It still seems as good as any.

$\mathbf{\mathit{+}}$

LEIF EIRIKSSON's assistance to his brother Thorvald's Vinland expedition didn't end with the loan of his well-tried *knarr*. In addition he gave him full sailing directions and also the free use of the shelters that he and his men had erected for their own winter stopover.

Thorvald shipped the usual complement of thirty men and bowled away before a fair wind in the spring of the year with a heart full of ambition. Whilst the saga doesn't enlarge upon the sort of trip he had, it does imply that by the time he reached Leif's shelters the season was getting on for winter. This makes sense. With a following wind, a chart, a sextant and a chronometer, a modern mariner could make the passage from Eiriksfjord to Newfoundland in five days. It wasn't like that for Thorvald Eiriksson.

To the casual twentieth-century eye, used to seeing Greenland and maritime Canada on a one-page map, the area seems small and tight. Not so to Thorvald. He sailed from Eiriksfjord with no compass, no log, no conception of the idea of longitude and without having ever seen a chart of any sort. His task was to find two or three turf houses camouflaged against their background somewhere in a land to the south and west. Anyone who has ever arrived out of the bowl of the ocean and been confronted with the infinite possibilities of a continent he has never before visited will understand what took Thorvald so long.

Once they had found the place, however, everything went smoothly for a while. Like Leif, Thorvald met up with no indigenous inhabitants at the Vinland camp and he and the crew passed a peaceful winter. When spring came round all hands were anxious to explore, rather than merely stock up and go home, and this is where their luck ran out.

For all Eirik's propaganda machine, Greenland was a pretty grim spot compared with a place like Vinland. So, perhaps with a view to beginning a colony of their own, the travellers cast around for a suitable site to settle. The immediate vicinity of Leif's shelters evidently left something to be desired.

Their first misfortune was the uncomplicated matter of a shipwreck. While coasting to the east and north they found themselves pinned on a lee shore by a vicious storm. Despite their efforts to save their ship they were driven up the beach close to a prominent headland. Inspection of the ship revealed that her back was broken. Their voyage could have ended there and then, but these men were not quitters.

After sizing up the problem they spat on their hands and found that they were able to effect a repair by replacing the whole keel.

The job dragged, but finally it was completed to the satisfaction of the ship's carpenter and on they sailed. One saga has it that they erected the old keel as a monument and called the place Keel-ness. Well, perhaps they did.

The second mishap suffered by the expedition demonstrates a principle reason for the failure of the Norse to successfully colonise North America. They came up against some locals, and straightaway committed a major indiscretion.

Shortly after selecting a place for his future homestead, Thorvald discovered nine men of an unknown race sleeping under canoes on the foreshore. Instead of waking them gently and offering them a smoke and a beer, his men captured them, or at least they tried to. In the ensuing scuffle one of them escaped. Thorvald then perpetrated his fatal act of folly. True to type, he resorted to battleaxe diplomacy and had the eight prisoners summarily slain.

It wasn't long before the forces of retribution came paddling round a corner. A seemingly endless procession of canoes was approaching. The natives were making ugly gestures and were clearly not calling with an invitation to take afternoon tea, so Thorvald and his worthies retreated in close order to the ship. Once aboard they hurriedly erected their shield wall around the bulwark. All aboriginal inhabitants of Greenland or North America were dubbed *skraelings* by the Norse. The term, which is one of contempt, means something like 'wretches', but on this, as on most other occasions when the two factions met, the *skraelings* had the last laugh, in spite of being called rude names.

In the brief skirmish that now took place, no-one was hurt except for Thorvald, who stopped an arrow that slipped between two shields. In a classic Viking death speech, he announced to his followers that although there was plenty of fat round his guts the wound would be the death of him. He then instructed them, with a fine sense of irony, to bury his bones on the site he had chosen for his homestead because, as he managed to gasp before he expired, 'It looks as though I was right when I said I might dwell here for a time.'

While Thorvald's ill-fated journey was running its course, Leif the Lucky had not been idle. His Vinland voyage had established him locally but he realised that if he was ever to measure up to his father's prestige, he still had plenty to do. The time had come to consolidate.

During the period of Leif's trip to America, a Viking sea-lord by the name of Olaf Trygvasson had become King of Norway. In order to subjugate the chiefs this imaginative man had indulged in the sort of old-fashioned atrocities not seen for decades, and he had gone one better than any of his predecessors: he had butchered, tortured, burned and no doubt raped as well, 'in the name of Christ our Lord, Amen'.

This Leif had to see, and so at the first opportunity he shipped out bound for Norway and King Olaf's court. On passage he suffered the usual storms and ended up spending a winter of luxurious contentment in the Hebrides. Here, our storm-bound hero took up with a beautiful Celtic witch by the name of Thorgunna. In the spring, ignoring her entreaties, he sailed on to Norway, leaving her carrying his child. He finally arrived at the King's Hall where, buoyed up by the confidence gained from his personal achievements, he got on famously with Olaf, and learned something of his methods.

When it came to missionary work, Olaf's charms were irresistible. He had various ways of converting the heathen. A simple offer of death as an alternative to baptism was available to the masses, but was considered beneath the dignity of men of quality. For these, sundry special arguments were reserved; a sample of which is the doctrine of the serpent and the war horn.

The pagan was immobilised and the thin end of a hollow horn was rammed well down his throat. An adder was then introduced to the open mouth of the horn and a lid clamped on. If the beneficiary of this proselytising still resisted the Love of God, the missionary applied heat to the horn, encouraging the snake to leave by the only way open to it! Needless to say, there was a substantial number of converts.

This Christian monarch was one of the first to learn the full value of clerical support for his regime. Leif was, perhaps not surprisingly, readily converted to the Faith, and signed up to preach the gospel in Greenland. Realising the power that this mission could give him, he attacked his work with gusto as soon as he returned home.

It isn't hard to imagine what his Old Man thought about all this. One of the corner-stones of Eirik's operation had always been an honest relationship with Thor. Many of his senior colonists had joined him on the basis of escaping the creeping paralysis of the Monk-Seeker that was rife in Iceland. Now here was Leif, the child of Eirik's body, arriving back from the fleshpots challenging his authority in this most underhand of ways. A sinister sideline to the arrival of the monks with Leif and his followers was the implication of Olaf Trygvasson's sponsorship of the new deal.

'Monks this year,' Eirik probably thought to himself, 'Tryg-vasson's Vikings next. No. Thank you very much!' and he resolutely turned his back on this thinly-veiled threat to his independence.

The women, however, signed for the 'White Christ' lock, stock and barrel and Thjodhild, with whom Eirik had come through so much, slammed the door to her chamber in his face. He, Eirik the Red, direct descendant of Oxen-Thorir and High Chief of all Greenland, was confronted with a lock-out.

Eirik was so angry at this general ingratitude that when his youngest son Thorstein proposed that he join him on a Vinland trip, he needed little persuading. Many a good man has gone to sea to get away from his wife and Eirik made up his mind to be no exception.

The expedition certainly appeared to be well-starred. Thorstein was an extraordinary young man in every way, being quietly effective without having to resort to the flamboyant antics of his eldest brother. It says a lot for Thorstein that Gudrun Thorbjorns-dottir agreed to be his wife in spite of the presence of Leif the Lucky, the powerful, the successful, the established womaniser. Gudrun was the most eligible and desirable woman in Greenland at that time, having arrived with her father, Eirik's old partner Thorbjorn Vifilsson, a year or two before. She was descended from the Celtic Irish nobility and was not the sort of woman to be left at home while her menfolk sailed away to deeds of glory, so she determined to accompany Thorstein on his voyage.

When everyone was on board and the decision had been made to sail that day, word was sent to Eirik. With great pomp he strode from his hall and mounted his finest horse to ride to the ship. Halfway down the slope the beast shied and Eirik was thrown to the ground, sustaining minor damage to his rib cage and shoulder. This so demoralised him that he announced immediately that the voyage would be better proceeding without him. His luck had carried him so far, he said, but here was a sign, clear to all, that he should attempt to go no further. Whether this was his real motivation or whether he was simply concerned about going to sea with possibly undiagnosed internal injuries will never be known, but whatever Eirik's reasons for pulling out, Thorstein and Gudrun sailed without him.

They never stood a chance. All summer long they were storm-driven about the ocean, lost, starving, half-dead from cold and damp. At one point a prolonged south-westerly gale drove them to within sight of Iceland; they then managed to work south but the Gulf Stream took them so far to the eastwards that their pilot recognised birds that could only have come from Ireland. By now the summer was well advanced and any modern navigator could have told them that without some exceptionally good fortune they had no hope at all of bearing direct from Ireland to Vinland in what remained of the sailing season.

They tried nonetheless but finally, with their morale shattered and with a depleted ship's company, they limped back into the Greenland Sea. Once more a southerly gale carried them before it, and just before the winter night descended they made landfall at what was known as the Western Settlement. This was the overspill colony several hundred miles up the west Greenland coast from the Eiriksfjord area.

Here they spent a bizarre winter in the home of a friend of the family called Thorstein the Black. Plague broke out and people died off with shocking regularity. Thorstein Eiriksson himself perished as did the wife of Thorstein the Black, but death did not quieten their spirits. The dead walked in the longhouses all that Arctic winter. They would not lie down. The corpse of Eiriksson rose up and prophesied that his wife's future lay with an Icelander. As the tallow lamps guttered and fumed and the Polar gales howled in the dark outside, Sigrid, the wife of Thorstein the Black, could find no rest. Days after her pulse had ceased and her breath was gone she was found trying to climb into someone else's bed. Poor Thorstein had no choice but to drive an axe into the breast of his undead wife; this, it seems, did the trick.

When this nightmare finale to the third Vinland voyage ground to its ghastly close with the end of that dreadful winter, Gudrun and Thorstein the Black piled the bodies into a ship and sailed down to Eiriksfjord. How they held onto their sanity through those endless bitter nights is difficult to conceive, but hold onto it they did.

They were well received by Eirik, who took Gudrun into his care and fixed up Thorstein the Black with a useful smallholding, where he quietly lived out his days enjoying the universal respect of the community.

By now, Gudrun must have been an impressive woman. Although still childless she had survived two husbands and she had witnessed enough death and trauma in the previous twelve months to last her a lifetime. She was proud, singleminded and still determined to travel onward to Vinland, but she was prepared to wait until she found the right man to partner her.

She bided her time all through the following winter and there is no record of any young man having had the nerve to approach her until the summer after she and Thorstein the Black had sailed into Eiriksfjord from the north-west, when two strange *knarrs* came

around the headland, and anchored below Eirik's hall. The senior captain was a man called Thorfinn Karlsefni, a well-known and high-born Icelandic merchant adventurer. As he and his men strode ashore, still smelling of the sea, Gudrun watched them carefully. They would stay until spring – that was the custom – so she would have plenty of time to consider them and to decide whether or not they were tied up with the prophesy of the dead Thorstein Eiriksson.

(*opposite*) *John Lovell shaping up a new board for the cabin sole*

Ice, the swear box and more wicked weather

'THERE goes our last chance of an ice report,' said Ros as the Russians left us to our fate. 'So what are we going to do, Thomas?'

I looked at the sky where, for the second time that day, the sun was visible behind the thin layer of cloud. 'The first thing is to find out where we are,' I replied just as Patrick emerged from the companionway with his sextant. 'We managed one sun line at breakfast time. Pat says it tallies with the dead reckoning, so another sight now should set us up with a reasonable position.'

Because the cloud cover was making the job tricky Patrick and I each took an observation. As always, the shades on the sextant mirrors miraculously focused the hazy sun into a sharp sphere, and we were able to obtain position lines which plotted only one mile apart from one another. We studied the fix on the chart and saw that it was about ninety miles east-north-east of Cape Farewell. The wind was now south-east Force 4 and *Hirta* was sailing well. There was only one thing to do.

'We'll go in closer and take a look,' I said shortly, and shaped a course to a point forty miles south of the headland. 'That will put us where the ice edge was when we left Reykjavik. The pack must surely have moved in the last two weeks. If there's no sign of ice when we arrive and the weather's fair we can head in some more. If there is still ice in the offing, or the wind is piping up . . . well, we'll see when we get there.'

That evening we had supper in the cockpit for the first time since the day of the dolphin circus just west of Iceland. John and Mike took over at eight o'clock and the sun set half an hour later. Halfway through the four-hour watch there was still enough twilight left to be able to read the water.

'There seems to be quite a swell coming in from the south,' John observed as *Hirta* lifted bodily to a long, high wave. 'What was the barometer doing when you entered the log book, Mike?'

'Nothing at all,' was the reply. 'It's steady at 1008. Have you seen the moon, though?'

We turned to look. The daylight had faded sufficiently for it to be visible high up behind our shoulders. Like the sun earlier in the day, the moon could just be seen through the ever-present sheet of thin cloud. The interesting feature was the halo that stood out in a full circle well clear of it.

I looked at John's face. It was a picture. 'Looks like horrors for lunch tomorrow,' was all he said. I decided to turn in then and enjoy the saloon berth which for once was dry as well as warm. As I walked past the chart table I gave the barometer a friendly tap. Its blank face stared back at me insolently and it remained stolidly on 1008. Just for luck I rapped the glass once more. The needle dipped half a point which, at eleven at night within fifty miles of the Greenland pack, was all that was needed to ensure that dreamland would be filled with hateful fantasies of disaster.

The final decision about whether to try for Eiriksfjord or work our way on to Newfoundland was taken in the middle of the afternoon watch next day.

Patrick and Chris were catching up on their sleep, Mike was keeping Hannah amused in her lair and John, Ros and myself were gathered around the wheel, looking to the north. By now the wind was hardening from a point east of south and the swell was growing steeper. The barometer had fallen steadily all night and was still dropping.

Directly to leeward of us, low down in the far distance, lay a remarkable bank of stable, dark-grey cloud. John was staring at it through the binoculars. He handed them to me and pointed to an area to the right of the centre of the cloud. I adjusted the focus and found the place he had indicated. There, jutting dramatically through the vapour, were two jagged snow-covered peaks.

I gazed at them in fascination until my eyes ached. Then I passed the glasses to Ros.

'There they are,' I said reverently. 'That's the high land that Leif put over his stern-post when he sailed for Vinland. Bjarni probably raised those mountains when he finally came in down his latitude from the west. God knows how many others . . .'

'Never mind Leif and Bjarni,' said Ros, irritated by my romanticising, 'what's Tom Cunliffe going to do?' And she glanced meaningfully into the eye of the rising wind.

There was no ice in sight but right across the sky between us and the cloud that we now knew was hanging over the Greenland ice cap was a bright glare that had to be a reflection of some sort.

'Do you suppose that's ice blink, John?' I had never seen this phenomenon before.

'I'm damn sure it is,' he replied. 'That's a definite sign that there is heavy pack ice not too far away. Cape Farewell is only just below the horizon so there must still be plenty of pack coming round the corner.'

'Hell.'

'The wind's in the south,' Ros offered heroically, 'so we could always run up the Davis Strait until we reached the north end of the tongue of ice, assuming it's clinging to the coast. Then perhaps the wind will have changed and we can work down the shore-lead into Eiriksfjord. How far did Thor Jakobsson say the pack could extend to the north-west of the Cape?'

'Two to three hundred miles.'

'H'mmm . . . even with this wind that'd be two or three days. Once we get near to the ice edge we'll have to slow down. Then it'll be another three days to work through the growlers down the shorelead . . .'

'What's a growler, Mummy?' Hannah popped up, followed by Mike who, obscurely, was carrying a large pipe wrench.

'A growler's a baby iceberg. It floats right down in the water and you can't see it easily. They're very dangerous.'

'Oooh!' squeaked Hannah gleefully and began conducting a one-child growler watch, staring into the freezing wind until her little eyes watered.

'So there's no chance of pushing through to the fjords in much less than a week.' John brought the meeting to order. 'Then if the ice stays where it is it'll be another week to get out again . . . It could be nearly September before we make it even as far as Newfoundland.'

I was coming rapidly to a decision. 'There's something else to consider,' I pointed out. 'This air that's blowing now is far colder than it ought to be coming from the south, and it's flowing straight from the Gulf Stream, so it's chock full of moisture. You can feel the damp in it. It'll only take a degree or two drop in sea temperature and we'll have some champion fog. There's ice a few miles to leeward, and that cloud over the land mass is really spelling out the message. If we press on to the north-west and head for the Davis Strait, we could find ourselves in a whole gale on a lee shore of uncharted ice, with dense fog for a sideshow because the water will be much colder than it is here, once the ice gets really close.'

'What do we do then, give it a miss?' Mike enquired expressionlessly.

For a few seconds more I pondered, but the wind was breezing up every minute and the sky to windward was thickening noticeably. I looked once more at the ice blink, and shivered.

'Bring her up to the wind, John. Let's see if we can lay the Belle Isle Strait!'

'That's it then, is it?' he asked. 'Goodbye Greenland.'

I examined his expression. The decision was a serious disappointment to me and I had no way of knowing how the rest of the ship's company would feel. I nodded glumly by way of response.

'Thank God for that,' he breathed 'I was afraid you wouldn't see sense.' He brought *Hirta* up to a south-west heading and Mike hardened the sheets as

Hannah sports her sub-Arctic sailing gear

the spray began to fly once more. Ros and Hannah retreated to the galley to brew the tea, and John steered comfortably into the steep seas. He sensed my need for reassurance. 'Really, there was no other decision you could have made,' he said. 'It's going to blow like a bandit before midnight and anyone caught down there in the ice could easily end up camping on an iceberg. In any case, the Labrador Sea in September isn't much of a temptation to anyone.

'Don't worry about Patrick,' he went on, voicing my innermost anxiety. 'He'll be disappointed, just like you, but he'll go along with the decision happily enough. The weather never gave us a break.'

Just then *Hirta* butted her shoulder into a breaking wave and bitterly cold spray soaked us both with a sickening 'splat'. I thought of Thorstein Eriksson and his bride and what happened to them, and began to count my blessings.

The six-hundred-mile passage from the vicinity of Cape Farewell down to Cape Bauld at the northern tip of the Island of Newfoundland proved to be much faster than the preceding six hundred miles from Iceland. We didn't manage it in the five *doegr* which would have been comfortable for us in fair weather, but we ran it off in just over a week.

John's predictions about the weather prospects proved to be correct. By midnight the wind was up to Force 8 and all hands were deep-reefing the main as a beastly cold sleet sucked the warmth from our fingers. Our combined strength was not enough to tie in the central reef-points and so Mike suggested a system which became known as the 'sharp stick'. This worked beautifully. One man on the windward side shoved a 3ft-long broom handle between the boom and the bunt of the sail. He then bore down on his end of it and his weight served to lever the bunt of frozen sailcloth into submission. The reef-point nearest the stick could then be tied by whoever had drawn the short straw and was stationed down to leeward. This position was doubly undesirable because not only did the victim rip his hands to pieces on the icy reef-points, he was also in real danger of being prodded in the face by the stick.

In the weight of wind she was getting *Hirta* was able to make 4 knots in the right direction even without a jib set, but how she was missing her spitfire! For days there was no chance of setting the big jib because it would have certainly damaged either itself or the ship in the permanent Force 6 breezes. A gaff cutter will sail adequately, though not powerfully, with jib and main only. Under staysail and main with no jib she is unbalanced and cumbersome. If the wind is well aft and there is plenty of it, she will sail along well enough, but if it is forward of the beam she desperately needs a jib, even a tiny one. And so we slugged it out.

Whales became such frequent callers that after a while the watch below didn't bother to turn out and pay their respects. 'Thar she blooows!' The thrilling age-old cry from the deck was greeted with only muffled oaths and groans.

After fifteen days of the sort of frustration, pain and grief that we all had to put up with, the question of 'swearing in front of the children' was becoming a thorny problem. It was solved by Ros with a move of pure genius.

'Right, boys,' she announced to the assembled male contingent, after serving us a notable breakfast of potatoes, onions and eggs fried up in butter. 'Here's how it's going to be: we've having a swear box from now on. You can curse and rave as much as you like, but if Hannah hears you, she's going to charge you a penny a word. That way, she'll know people aren't really supposed to talk like you lot. I've told her what the naughty words are. I've also explained that if the grown-ups try to stop saying them they'll probably end up with psychological problems and have to go to hospital, but from now on, she's the ship's Morality Officer. Curse you may, but pay you must!'

Patrick took a gulp of his coffee. 'That's a bloody good idea,' he said thoughtfully.

'One penny please,' piped a small voice.

By the time we tied up in Newfoundland the box was already full enough to make a useful contribution to a charity of Hannah's choice.

As *Hirta* worked her way south and west we began to be concerned about bergs coming down on the Labrador Current. These huge ice islands are not members of the same family as the Cape Farewell pack. They are shore ice, generally calved from the mighty glaciers of northern Greenland. After they hit the sea, they may float around the upper reaches of Baffin Bay for many years before finally drifting into the south-flowing current. Once caught up in this, however, they are as good as finished. It carries them southwards relentlessly, especially in the summer months, until they either run aground and disintegrate off the coast of southern Labrador, or make their way to the Grand Banks where they meet the Gulf Stream water. Here they rapidly melt, and all the detritus they have picked up in Greenland before they fell from the glacier wall is dumped onto the ocean floor, adding with infinite slowness to the ever-increasing shoals which are their only legacy.

The nights were rapidly lengthening as we piled up our southing. So long as visibility was reasonable, the dark hours were the only time that the potential for meeting icebergs was a problem. Unfortunately, as we approached the current of Arctic water the fog came back to pester us. One evening as the watch was changing at eight o'clock all hands were on deck.

'How's it been?' asked Chris, who was wondering whether or not to risk

Ice in the Labrador Sea, with grey seas and half a gale

soaking the dead-sheep coat, and suffer the resulting stench. Mike had taken the second dog watch looking like a character from an advertisement for 'Sunshine Holidays in Casablanca'. He thought wearing shorts would make a refreshing change, he had said, but his reply to Chris was unambiguous. 'Cold,' he said flatly. 'And very, very wet.'

Hirta, for once, was logging 6 knots on a close reach. I was reluctant to slow her down but the danger of running into a growler or even a berg in the foggy darkness was becoming acute. The only way that we could responsibly carry on at such a speed would be to station a look-out on the foredeck. He would be able to see what was coming, but he was going to have a tough time of it because the deck forward of the mast was being constantly swept by freezing spray. Patrick, who together with Mike formed the 'feel-no-pain' contingent, came up with the solution.

'Why don't we go onto a half-hour crash watch system?' he suggested. 'Half an hour on the foredeck, half an hour as teaboy, half an hour on the helm, then one hour in the sack, and back to the foredeck again. Ros can stay out of it, but the five of us should be able to keep that up for twenty-four hours easily. By then, perhaps things will have improved.'

'You first on the foredeck, then!' said Chris amicably, 'and I'll volunteer for an hour in the quarter-berth.'

Ignoring this handsome offer we sent Chris forward. Following Mike's advice he had struggled into an ancient and threadbare oilskin, the dead-sheep took a dry watch in the quarter-berth, where the atmosphere was less smelly than it might otherwise have been. The rest of us settled into Pat's routine, which the committee passed unanimously as being a sound one. Agonising though the foredeck watch was, no-one wanted us to slacken our pace, now that we were finally gobbling up the *doegrs*.

Mike was official teaboy when it was my first trick at the wheel. He served up the Bovril, pumped the bilge, and then stood on the bottom step of the accommodation ladder looking aft towards where I was trying to duck the flying water.

'This excavated site we're headed for,' he began, 'what makes you so sure it's Vinland?'

'Actually, I'm not sure that it's Vinland at all. I think it's much more likely to be a camp used for wintering by one of the later expeditions; perhaps it was some unsung Norse woodcutter who never made it to saga status. No-one will ever know exactly where Leif's Vinland was.'

Mike guzzled his drink. 'And you're content with that for a destination, are you?' he asked.

'Completely,' I retorted, 'because the point is that the place is undisputably a Norse settlement. It's the only one definitely identified anywhere on the North American continent. We've got to make our target somewhere, so rather than get involved in a load of academic argument about where Vinland was, or was not, what better result then to fetch up at the one place that we know beyond doubt was visited by the Greenland *knarrs?*'

I saw him nod in the dim glow of the binnacle light. 'I wonder what it'll be like?' he said simply.

That was the first time any of us had risked 'putting the mouth' on our safe arrival by openly discussing it. On an average mid-latitude ocean voyage there comes a point somewhere in the middle where you stop talking about the place you've left and begin speculating about the one you are going to. This passage had been different, but suddenly we all felt that we were nearly there and the unspoken taboo was at last breaking down.

The following morning visibility increased to a couple of miles and immediately Chris, who had the watch, saw the ice. Directly in our path lay an enormous berg, 200ft (62m) high and a quarter of a mile (400m) long. The seas were crashing into its weather side and all round it growlers and bergy bits were dancing like strobe-lit groupies. We bore away to give it a wide berth and no sooner were we past it than the fog closed in once more.

The impact on all of us of seeing this great ghostly mountain of ice sailing towards its inevitable end on the Grand Banks was considerable. The thing had been in existence up in the wild Arctic regions for thousands, perhaps million of years and was, as like as not, unseen by man all that time. Now on

Labels on the map:
LABRADOR
NEWFOUNDLAND

LABRADOR

STRAIT

Belle Isle

l'Anse aux Meadows site

ISLE

BELLE

GULF OF ST LAWRENCE

NEWFOUNDLAND

NORTH
ATLANTIC
OCEAN

**Belle Isle Strait and
l'Anse aux Meadows site**

*The Belle Isle Strait and l'Anse aux Meadows site. The
chart shows clearly how the Strait resembles the mouth of
an immense fjord and could easily have been taken for one
by the Norse and named Straumfjord out of respect for the
strong tides which run to this day*

its final voyage, it had briefly crossed the path of seven people sailing on a dream. Maybe nobody else would set eyes on it before it finally dissolved back into the ocean, but before we had time to develop any beautiful thoughts on the question, Mike brought us back to reality.

'Good thing we didn't hit that,' he said, stating the obvious. 'We'd better wire Chris up to the ship's mains to keep him awake on the foredeck tonight. Now we've seen the enemy . . .'

'I keep awake quite adequately by thinking filthy thoughts, thank you very much,' retorted Chris. 'It's you that needs . . .'

'One penny, please,' demanded Hannah looking Chris defiantly in the eye.

'Waddaya mean, one penny? My language, as always, is clean and pure.'

'You had filthy thoughts. Mummy say that's more than good enough for a penny.'

Chris looked black but, rather than risk short rations from arguing with Ros, he paid up like a gentleman.

Two days after this with *Hirta* an estimated fifty miles from Cape Bauld, John managed to tune our long-wave domestic radio into the Canadian weather forecast for shipping. After spending a long time down by the chart table he emerged and scrutinised the sky astern. Not having seen the sun, moon or stars for four days our position was now in considerable doubt. His announcement was about to make this even more relevant.

'Guess what, boys and girls?'

'OK. Let's have it!'

'Easterly gale, Force 9, within the next twelve hours!'

'You're joking!'

'No, I'm not.' And we could see that he wasn't. The wind had backed right round to the south-east and the barometer had been falling all day as we enjoyed our first truly fair wind of the trip. *Hirta* was clicking the miles off in grand style and we had been vainly anticipating a painless end to the voyage. This was the worst news the weathermen could have given us. We could not risk being caught on a lee shore in the permanently thick visibility while we were unsure of our position. We had come too far to pile up now.

'Is it worth giving the RDF another try?' asked Ros. Patrick and I had been persevering with this for the past twenty-four hours and had achieved scant success.

'We'll give it another whirl in a few hours, but the beacons are feeble,' I said. I was feeling positively petulant that the wind, which had stayed so resolutely in the west all the way from Iceland, should appear to relent at the last minute, and then give our tail such a savage twist. For a while I stomped around the deck snarling indiscriminately at anyone in my way. If there had been a cat I would have kicked it. All the time I peered skywards, but no clearance was to be seen. We guessed that visibility was about two miles. It seemed that I was beyond making any sort of decision, even though the

201

choice was a simple one. Should we heave-to and stay put with what was, in all likelihood, a safe offing, or should we press on and hope for the best?

John came quietly forward to where I was sulking on the foredeck. The rest of the hands in the cockpit were trying unsuccessfully to appear disinterested.

'I think, Skip,' John said gently, 'that the only thing you can do is keep going and make the most of the wind before it gets too strong. If you heave-to now the boys won't be happy . . . in fact, they'll be very unhappy. We can always hang about later if it really does blow hard – and, you never know, we might get a sight in half an hour . . .'

I glanced surreptitiously at the sombre faces around the wheel. John obviously had his finger on the collective pulse of the ship's company.

'All right, then,' I decided. 'We'll blast on, but God help us if Belle Isle suddenly comes up on the end of the bowsprit in a Force 9.'

So we ran on until dark and saw nothing at all. Visibility stayed as it was but as night began to fall the gale suddenly came tearing down onto us and we hove-to with double-reefed main and staysail in Force 8. Soon after dark a fearsome gust swept over the ship making her heel her rail right under the water. This is unheard of in *Hirta* when she is hove-to and straightaway the watch called for all hands.

The rain was driving horizontally across the deck as we crept forward to go for the deep reef. There was so much water in the air, rain mixed with spray, that it was hard to discern the end of the boom from the mast, but somewhere down aft Chris and Patrick were hooking the deep-reef pennant onto the heavy block of the reefing tackle. John had eased the throat halyard and Mike and I were wrestling with the tack. By the time we had set it up a thin voice was calling from the living darkness twenty feet away, 'OK boys, haul it down!'

Mike, John and I tailed onto the fall of the reefing tackle to pull down the clew but we weren't winning. Pat struggled forward to help us out; Chris stood by to cram the bight onto the pin and Ros, who had materialised on deck from her dry bunk, was calling the shots from the boom end.

I took a deep breath. 'One, two-six – heavieee!' The clew cringle came in a little. 'Two-six – heavieee!' Another wild shout. Another six inches, and so on until finally, when our arms were cracking with the strain, Ros' voice, high against the storm, 'That'll do!'

Chris grabbed the bight of the pennant. 'Stand by . . . Slack up!' he yelled sharply and we all let go as he skilfully slammed a turn around the belaying pin on the mast. Now all we had to do was tie in the points.

'Hey, Chris! How would you like a poke in the eye with a sharp stick?'

'Get stuffed!'

It sounded as though morale was back to normal, but somewhere out in the roaring dark to leeward was Belle Isle, ironbound and hungry. The question was, where?

Genocide in Vinland
by Eirik's evil daughter

THE last two documented Viking expeditions to Vinland are so interwoven in the saga accounts that it seems impossible to discern whether they were, in fact, separate voyages, or were both part of the same overall venture.

The story of Thorfinn Karlsefni shows him, as we would expect for a man of his reputation, to be a dedicated professional of Bjarni Herjolfsson's calibre. He was an example of that rarest type of Norseman, a genuine explorer with a thirst for knowledge. There is no difficulty in placing his voyage on the calendar of the crossings to North America, as the timing we are given fits in neatly with other contemporary events.

The second voyage is more apocryphal. It may have been a branch of the Karlsefni expedition, though it appears more probable that it was a separate voyage in its own right. The important feature of this effort was that, lacking the sort of strong lead offered by the prime movers of the other western voyages, it degenerated into a sordid catalogue of vice and butchery. It was headed by a lady called Freydis, who was yet another of Eirik the Red's children, but this time from the wrong side of the sheets.

The ship that arrived in Eiriksfjord alongside Thorfinn Karlsefni's the summer after Gudrun's return was a *knarr* belonging to the Icelandic trading partners Thorhall Gamlasson and Bjarni Grimolfsson. Together with Karlsefni they brought their goods and their gear into Eirik's barns to store for the winter and the whole group signed up as house guests of the great man.

The fact that one of Karlsefni's forebears was Thord Bellower, a supporter of Thorgest of Breidabolstead, Eirik's old enemy, is a definite indication that, for once, the settlement made between two Viking chiefs over a series of killings was being upheld. There is no suggestion of anything but the most cordial relations between Eirik and his main guest. Like Gudrun, Thorfinn had Celtic blood in his veins. His progenitor on his great-grandmother's side was Kiarval, a High King of Ireland, while his great grandfather traced his descent from such famous names as Bjorn Chestbutter, Thorvald Backbone and Bjorn Ironsides through to the great Ragnar Shaggypants himself.

A merry time was had by all in Eirik's longhouse below the hill that winter. There was an uneasy lull in the proceedings just before Christmas when Eirik realised that he was about to run out of beer, but Karlsefni and the partners immediately offered him a gift of the makings, which they just happened to have in their cargoes! From then on, festivities went with a swing and the dark weeks passed in an orgy of chess-playing, friendly wrestling bouts, boasting and yarn-spinning.

At some stage during this six-month party Gudrun made up her mind about her future and in no time at all she was married to Thorfinn Karlsefni. As usual, talk over the festive board turned to good times and bad far away in Vinland which, by this time, had taken on the status of a promised land. Those who had visited the place and been spared by the sea and the *skraelings* told tales of salmon the size of full-grown codfish, of antelope as big as elephants and of dew that tasted sweeter than wine. Karlsefni began to consider putting up the ships and money for a proper exploration with the defined purpose of establishing a colony in this new world. In spite of her terrible experiences of the North Atlantic, Gudrun was still fired with enthusiasm to journey to Vinland, and she worked steadily on her husband until, by springtime, he was as keen as anyone to put out to sea.

In the end, both Icelandic *knarrs* set sail on what was a thoroughly well-found expedition. Instead of simply blasting off to the south-west as the others had done, Karlsefni and Gudrun followed the more conventional Viking system of navigation and hugged the coast wherever possible. By now, the west Greenland shore and the Baffin Island peninsulas were well explored by hunting expeditions so the ships began their odyssey by sailing north and then west. From a small island off the Baffin coast which they called Bear Island, they sailed south to Labrador and Bjarni Herolfsson's departure point on the same latitude as Cape Farewell.

Once they had arrived at what we know, but they did not, to be the American mainland, they ran south down the Labrador coast, exploring and giving names to the different areas. When they reached the valuable forests they called the place Markland before pressing on to the south.

Somewhere in southern Labrador or northern Newfoundland they established a base camp at the mouth of a huge fjord with an island at its seaward entrance. Tidal streams ran rapidly here and they gave the place the name Straumfjord. This place was inhabited off and on for three years, and may well have been used by Freydis and her motley crew soon afterwards. Like every other named location in these sagas, it is impossible for us to be sure of where it was, but it is at least arguable that the Straumfjord camp is the site which has been excavated in l'Anse aux Meadows, a few miles to the westward of Cape Bauld on the Belle Isle Strait.

The first winter was a tough one. Expecting a better deal from the weather, the explorers had not laid in adequate supplies, having instead spent their time cutting timber for a cargo and stacking it properly to season. By doing this they had secured the financial success of the venture but, as they now discovered, you cannot eat money.

In the depths of winter they became desperate for food and many of them began praying to Christ and the Virgin for a herd of game, a stranded whale, or some other windfall. Thorhall the Hunter, a tough old backwoodsman sent by Eirik to accompany the voyagers, would have nothing to do with this defeatist practice. Instead he made known his demands to Thor who, he averred, had never let him down in the past. Sure enough, the next day a whale was found on the beach and all hands tucked in with a will. While they were still gorging themselves, old Thorhall was already making unfair comparisons between the benefits of Christianity and faithfulness to 'Redbeard', his familiar name for the Hammer God. He soon stopped his crowing, however, because by morning everyone in the camp, including himself, was seized with agonising stomach cramps and was throwing up, wishing only for the release of death.

Shortly after this unfortunate gastronomic affair Gudrun gave birth to a fine son, who she and Thorfinn named Snorri. He was the first child of European stock to be born in America. It was to be fully five hundred years before another would enter the record book.

In the springtime the religious differences of the factions of the expedition caused a confrontation. It was obvious that the conditions they had experienced so far were not as advertised in Leif's travel brochure, so it was necessary for them to explore further. Thorhall and his pagans were for going north, but Karlsefni felt, quite reasonably, that things were likely to be softer down to

205

the south, so with many hard words the two parties split up. Since the majority elected to stick with Karlsefni, the grand old Viking Thorhall and nine other reprobates took one of the small boats (about 25ft long) and disappeared in the direction from which they had come.

Thorhall, always ready with a quick stanza, ran off a verse or two about how he had been led astray:

> These oak-hearted warriors
> Lured me to this land
> With promise of choice drinks;
> Now I could curse this country!
> For I, the helmet-wearer,
> Must now grovel at a spring
> And wield a water-pail;
> No wine has touched my lips.

(*from* The Vinland Sagas,
Magnus Magnusson & Hermann Pálsson)

His literary efforts did him no good, however, because soon his boat was caught up in the Gulf Stream and the predictable westerly gales. After having its will with them for some time the 'old, grey widowmaker', as men of Thorhall's ilk liked to call the sea, dumped them on a beach in western Ireland. Here they were soundly beaten up and sold into slavery. Thorhall the Hunter, unable to bear the humiliation, died shortly afterwards.

Karslefni, Gudrun and the rest found several promising sites for a colony, but always managed to fall foul of the *skraelings*. Like the New England settlers centuries later, they made some effort to trade and live peacefully alongside the Indians to the advantage of both communities, but it seemed that whatever they did, there was always a misunderstanding on one side or the other. The difference was in the outcome of these misunderstandings. In spite of their undoubted courage and their uncompromising nature, the Norsemen simply could not prevail without the benefits of firearms and the eventual overwhelming numbers which the settlers of a later age could muster.

This most promising of all the Norse expeditions kept up the unequal struggle with the rightful owners of this great land for another two years before finally throwing in the towel. By the time his parents left to return to Greenland, young Snorri was breeched, toddling around and, as like as not, receiving early lessons in swordplay. His first major sea voyage, like everything else his father organised except the Vinland venture, went without a hitch. After breaking their journey at Markland, Gudrun and Karlsefni returned to Eiriksfjord intact, before sailing back to Iceland the following year. There they prospered and to this day there are Icelanders who trace their ancestry back to this remarkable couple.

Bjarni Grimolfsson and Thorhall Gamlasson, the other half of the expedition, did not enjoy such a happy homeward journey. Halfway across the Labrador Sea it became clear that their ship-maintenance programme had not been as effective as they would have wished. The *knarr* was worm-eaten to the point of sinking.

In the absence of any workable pumping arrangements the Viking seafarers used buckets to keep the ocean where it belonged. In the centre of a *knarr* was a well in which the bilgewater collected. It was perfectly normal for two or three men to be employed bailing this continually in heavy weather because, not only did the ships inevitably leak as they worked, but also considerable quantities of water slopped in over the side.

Bjarni, Thorhall and their men were doing fine with the buckets in moderate weather and were encouraged that, in spite of the state of the ship, they would make it home, but once it came on to blow and the sea piled up in heaps all round them, they realised that they were sunk.

With the old *knarr* almost awash they launched the ship's boat. This was similar to the twenty-five footer in which Thorhall the Hunter and his heathens had successfully, if unwillingly, crossed the Atlantic two years before, but which could not be expected to accommodate the whole ship's company. After an unmanly struggle for places broke out, Bjarni suggested that the honourable thing to do would be to draw lots so that all would have an equal chance to be saved, regardless of rank, or muscle power. This appealed to the fatalistic Vikings and Bjarni must have been delighted to draw one of the long straws. Everyone accepted the judgement of the lottery except for one wretched young Icelander who began whining that Bjarni had promised his father that he would look after him.

'I've made my suggestion,' said Bjarni as the storm roared round them and the *knarr* creaked and lurched, unstable beneath its load of inrushing water. 'What's your idea?'

'Why don't you and I swop places?' was the youth's incredible reply. 'You climb back up here and I'll hop down into the boat. Then you won't have broken your word to my father.'

Bjarni's contempt for such cowardice was obvious, but he now realised that it was his fate to drown.

'If you are so afraid to die,' he sneered, 'that you are prepared to live for ever more in dishonour, I can do nothing more for you than

207

give you my place.' And he stepped back into the sinking *knarr.*

And so, somewhere on the ocean floor to the south of Cape Farewell, there lie the bones of a fine man. The ship's boat returned to Iceland. The *knarr* and her doomed crew were never seen again.

In the early spring of the year that Thorfinn Karlsefni, the ill-fated Bjarni Grimolfsson and the rest were returning to Greenland and Iceland, the last Vinland expedition to gain saga immortality put out to sea.

Freydis, an illegitimate daughter whose paternity Eirik the Red had acknowledged, was married to an unremarkable man called Thorvard. They farmed some land in Greenland known as Gardar.

Freydis Eiriksdottir was a powerful character. Like her father she was a dangerous person to cross and she had a notable partiality for getting her own way. When she decided to climb in on the family act and get rich quick in Vinland she enlisted the aid of two Icelandic brothers who were trading in Greenland. They had a *knarr.* Freydis seems to have borrowed Thorbjorn Vifilsson's and so, between them, they mounted a useful two-ship operation.

The deal was spelled out from the start. Fifty/fifty on the profits and, in order to ensure fair play, no more than thirty fighting men were to be shipped by either side. If this sounds an odd provision to make in an amicable partnership, subsequent events will show that whoever suggested it was already aware of the course affairs might take before the venture was over.

Freydis broke the rules before she ever left Greenland by signing on an extra five heavies and hiding them from the brothers. According to one account, Leif lent her his Vinland shelters to use during her visit but it appears just as likely that she ended up at Straumfjord, or even somewhere else altogether. Wherever it was that they wintered, the brothers got there first and loaded their stores into some ready-made huts. When Freydis arrived she immediately confronted the Icelanders and threw them out. The brothers, anxious to avoid trouble, built new longhouses for themselves nearby.

As was by now the normal procedure, the expedition's cargo of wood was cut and stacked before winter. The crews then laid up their ships and prepared for the long cold months ahead. It was common for personal animosities to flare up during these enforced periods of idleness, but this winter was worse than most. There was argument and threats of violence, the sports and games arranged between the two parties turned to squabbling and bickering and, before spring, all diplomatic relations had been severed.

The situation was very dangerous indeed, and it was now that Freydis showed her father's cunning. Her courage was never in doubt as is witnessed by an incident where the expedition was attacked by a vastly numerically superior band of *skraelings*. The Norsemen ran for cover under a hail of arrows but Freydis, who was pregnant, could not run fast enough. Instead she moved over to the body of a fallen Viking and picked up his broadsword. Then she turned to face the howling mob of *skraelings* who were pounding down on her, armed to the teeth. Just when it seemed she must go down, she ripped open her bodice and exposed her breasts to the oncoming Indians. This brought them up short, but when she began beating her bare flesh with the flat of the sword blade and advancing steadily upon them the *skraelings* broke ranks and ran away in a panic.

This, then, was the woman who confronted the Icelandic brothers and the men and women of their party early that spring.

For reasons of her own she wanted them all killed, but a pitched battle was going to be far too dangerous to her party. Repeated attempts to incite the gutless Thorvard to murder them in their beds met with no response and so she resorted to devious tactics to infuriate her menfolk. Early one morning she stole out of bed and walked about barefoot outside in the dewy grass. When her feet were thoroughly chilled she climbed back under the blankets and laid them on her husband.

'What's this?' he exclaimed. 'What have you been up to?'

Freydis then delivered her heart-thrust. 'If you are so blind that you cannot see that I've been out at the brothers' house, having my way with one of them, you aren't the man I took you for!'

The one thing guaranteed to rouse the passion of any Viking, even one so pitifully spineless as this Thorvard, was to tell him to his face that he was a cuckold. Thorvard woke up all the men in his house and crept across to the brothers' camp, where he took all the Icelanders prisoner. The luckless brothers and their followers were then dragged out one by one from the house and put to the sword on the spot. The bodies were thrown into a heap.

'Now what about the women?' asked Freydis meaningfully, but her men said that they weren't in the business of murdering women, which sounds very high-minded. In fact, since they hadn't enough women of their own this incident gave the bachelors among them a new interest in life which they weren't keen to lose.

Freydis, however, was more motivated by the delights of genocide than by considerations about the morale of her crew, and so she spoke up. 'Hand me an axe,' she rasped. Some weakling, probably her husband, who had nothing more to lose, passed her one of these heavy, wicked weapons. Without another word the wild, red-haired woman strode into the house. There was a flurry of activity, a few screams and the repeated sickening thud of the blade as it did its work and then Freydis reappeared, covered in blood, her eyes crazy with killing.

There were no more Icelanders in Vinland. Even the hardest case among her crew must have been sickened by this excess, and in a few more weeks they packed up and sailed back directly to Greenland.

Reflecting on her deeds during the return voyage, Freydis realised that her activities were going to lead to some heavy censure from her own people, and possibly some serious blood-feuding if news of them leaked through to Iceland. Somehow she had to ensure the silence of her followers. As the *knarrs* rolled northwards across the sea she began with threats. After having been given such a remarkable demonstration of her capabilities, her crew must have been impressed by Freydis' promises of instant death, but just to make sure, she finished off by handing out some handsome bribes.

In spite of all her efforts, her brother Leif smelt a rat and went in search of three of her men. Leif, it must be remembered, had studied under King Olaf Trygvasson who was one of the most creative torturers of his generation, and Freydis' poor sailors soon coughed up all they knew. From then on, this terrible woman was officially shunned by all, but it's impossible not to think that some of the older men must have borne a secret admiration for her singleminded pursuit of her own ends.

One way and another it was becoming obvious to the Norsemen of Greenland and Iceland that those who ventured down to Vinland had less than an even chance of coming home again. By about AD1010 they were starting to ask themselves whether or not the profits were worth the grief.

In fact, there is no record of a successful colony ever having been established by the Vikings in the New World but throughout the 300-year life of Norse Greenland it seems likely that voyages were being made at least as far as Markland to replenish stocks of timber. Those expeditions died out along with the remains of Eirik's dream as Norse energy began to wane and climatic conditions worsened in the fourteenth century, but by then, it was almost time for a new explorer called Christopher Columbus to sail westwards.

Journey's end

BY morning the easterly gale had blown itself out and, for a while, *Hirta* slopped around on the confused sea with not a breath of wind to steady her. Our dead reckoning position was now a circle of probability fifty miles across due to the unknown effect of the Labrador Current and our drift the previous night. At worst we had seventy miles to go to Cape Bauld and the Viking camp; at best we could be within twenty or twenty-five miles of it. The sun resolutely refused to show itself. We had fuel enough for fifty miles' motoring and we desperately needed to know where we were.

Patrick was determined not to be beaten by the RDF set, although I had had no luck with it all night. He was bent over the chart table in an attitude of devotion with the earphones clamped to his head. In one hand he was holding a giant marmalade sandwich and with the other he was sensitively tweaking the dials of the radio. After half an hour of private communication with the weird sounds of the beat frequency oscillator, he came on deck grinning in triumph.

'It looks as if we're in business,' he said happily. 'I can't hear a dickie bird from Belle Isle, but Cape Bauld is bearing due west. I've plotted the position line on the chart and it passes well clear of Belle Isle. There's nothing to hit between here and the beacon.'

'I wonder how far it is?' Mike wondered.

'Doesn't matter, really,' replied Pat. 'We're on the latitude; all we do now is run down it until we see something, just like Bjarni Herjolfsson. Actually the signal is quite strong, so I doubt it'll be more than thirty miles!'

'Whoopee!'

No sooner had we started the engine and set course than the wind came up out of the southwest and brought yet another reduction in visibility. We shook the reefs out of the mainsail, let draw both headsails and half an hour later the engine was shut down once more.

Pat was pleased about the wind because the radio set was useless with the diesel thumping away by his ear. An hour passed and he took another bearing. *Hirta* was now sailing at 6 knots.

'How's your course been, Mike?' he enquired.

'Spot on,' came the immediate reply from the helm. 'Due west, as ordered.'

'In that case, there's a hell of a current, or a mighty powerful tidal stream. The bearing's altered 10°. You'd better steer 285° for a bit.'

I joined Patrick at the chart table.

'If the bearing is changing that quickly, we must be pretty close in,' I observed. 'What do you reckon?'

'I'd say we'd less than twenty miles to go.'

'It can't be more than that. What a tide!'

'Maybe it's the mouth of Straumfjord.' Chris commented as he squeezed by. 'You can't help wondering, can you?'

'Are we going to be there today, then?' Mike wanted to know as we all trooped back to the cockpit. *Hirta* was sailing well now with her sheets slightly eased.

'I thought you liked it out here?'

'Not any more. I ate the last Mars bar at midnight!'

The next hour came round with an even more dramatic course alteration and an announcement from Patrick that the radio signal was extra loud. The breeze was falling away and visibility had closed to a thousand yards.

'I hope there are no rocks off the headland,' Ros grunted as she passed five mugs of tea up the hatch.

'No, we're quite safe approaching from this direction,' I reassured her. 'Once we see it, we can pass round it to the west side and keep the shore within sight until we get to Quirpon harbour entrance.'

We had chosen Quirpon for two reasons. The first was that on the chart it looked well-sheltered. The second was its proximity to l'Anse aux Meadows, the site of the old Norse settlement. We had no way of knowing that locally the harbour had an evil reputation.

I was on the point of taking a slurp of tea when Mike nudged me, so that I slopped it down the neck of my oilskins.

'Just up ahead there, Skipper,' he said confidentially, as I eyed him unlovingly, 'would that be it?'

I squinted into the mist beyond the bowsprit. He was right. In spite of his spectacles, Mike had sharp eyes.

'You saw it, you have the privilege . . .'

'LAND-HO!!'

Following this statement there was a general outbreak of tea-spilling, handshaking, back-slapping and other expressions of relief and merry-making. Hannah did a brisk trade with her naughty word box, although she was puzzled that the same vocabulary was used when everyone was happy as when we were all grizzling and frustrated.

Cape Bauld is a proper headland. It has a fine, rocky promontory, an old-fashioned lighthouse and a useful pointed hill immediately behind it. Once it was in clear view the rate at which the tide was setting us southward became obvious. We bore further and further away to the north to counteract its effect but we soon realised that we were losing ground as *Hirta* slowed down in the dying breeze.

We fired up the engine for the second time that day which gave *Hirta* sufficient speed to punch the tide and, by mid-morning, we were tied up at a small dock at the inner end of Quirpon harbour. The place looked like the dark side of the moon. Apart from the fish-house at the root of the jetty, the only sign of habitation was a group of shabby, one-storey dwellings half a mile down the beach. Between us and them the rubbish of all the world drifted listlessly on the breeze.

Across the quay from *Hirta* an old schooner was moored. Her stern was sawn off short, and she must have had a big engine, because her masts were cut down too far for her ever to sail for her living again. A bunch of decrepit characters were lounging around on the schooner and two square-rigged women wearing dungarees cut for comfort rather than speed were shuffling fish-boxes around the wharf in a desultory fashion. Just as in Iceland our arrival appeared to create not the slightest impression on the locals. A middle-aged gent wearing a checked shirt and a baseball hat pottered out of the fish-house and indicated wordlessly that we could lie where we were and, with that, communications began and ended.

'Where's the band?' demanded Chris.

'And what about the girls flocking to the pierhead?' snarled Mike.

'Shut up, and drink this!' ordered Ros and popped the cork of a bottle of champagne she'd been saving for the occasion. We poured this down our throats, followed it with a round from the bonded locker and began to feel better. Still the incumbents of the quay ignored us.

'D'you suppose the *skraelings* behaved like this crowd before they started shooting up Freydis and her lads?'

'I don't know, but if you think I'm about to perform a bosom-and-broadsword spectacular you're going to be disappointed.'

'It's probably the only way we'll get any reaction . . .'

Leaving this banter behind me I stepped unsteadily ashore and staggered into the fish-house in search of a telephone. I was having serious trouble finding my land-legs, and was helped not at all by the champagne and Scotch we had just consumed in lieu of elevenses. Inside the clapboard building the man who had given us the green light about tying up rose slowly out of a battered armchair from which several springs protruded. I asked him whether I could use his phone, and if he knew the number of Customs and Immigration. He looked at me as though I were weak in the head. 'Where you boys out of then?' he asked in a strange Scottish/Canadian accent.

'Iceland,' I replied proudly.

'Oh,' he said in a manner that implied that sailing vessels from there came

213

in every other day. 'Iceland, eh?' and he scrabbled in his pockets for a smoke. After lighting up he exhaled with a loud hiss, took off his hat and scratched his head. 'I shouldn't bother with them Customs, if I was you. They won't be interested.' Nor were they. When I finally made contact with the nearest officer, who proved to be the barber in a town many miles away, I was advised to enter further south and behave myself in the meantime.

Returning to *Hirta* to lower the yellow 'customs' flag, I found Ros and John deep in conversation with an old man puffing hard on a roll-up. The glue on his cigarette paper had failed untidily but he still persevered with the tattered remains. He was sitting on one of the oversized cleats to which *Hirta* was tied up. Significantly, the cleat was bent over and pulled halfway out of the dock; so, I noticed, were most of the others. The old boy was the captain of the schooner and he was spinning a yarn about how bad things had been in the harbour while *Hirta* was hove-to off Belle Isle the previous night. Boats had been sunk on their moorings and he indicated several washed up on the beach. He didn't know too much about this here 'Leef Erikswhatsisname' and he cared less, but he was certain that 'Karpoon' as he pronounced it was a desperate place to be caught in a north-easter. I looked again at the cleats and began to read their message.

All through that long afternoon as we tried to rest, visitors came wandering down to the dock. These callers would stand around coyly, pretending disinterest, before plucking up courage and opening the conversation. Each exchange of views and news was so similar to all the others that by teatime we were able to predict the parting shot and parry it with a neat, 'Looks like a bad place in a north-easter, this.'

'Yeah,' they said as they stumped off up the dock, robbed of their punch-line, 'none worse.'

An hour before sunset Chris and Pat who had slipped away after lunch in search of Vinland came roistering back down the dry dirt road. They were arm-in-arm with a pair of tough-looking individuals and were carrying the remains of a case of beer. With the assistance of these characters, who were fishermen from the neighbouring village of Griguet, they had found the Norse site and had thrown their temperance tickets into the Belle Isle Strait. All four came clattering aboard; the duty-free stores were broached and dinner was struck off the agenda.

Halfway through the evening Phillip Bridger, one of the Newfound-landers, disappeared. He returned after half an hour with his brothers, his melodian and more beer. After that there was no chance of putting the brakes on the proceedings and soon *Hirta*'s floorboards were rattling to the Newfoundland shuffle-dance and the gutsy music of Phillip's squeezebox.

(opposite) Griguet, Newfoundland

215

The boys from the schooner wandered across towards midnight and we had yarns of the dory fishing, more music and strong but steady drinking while the aurora burned up the sky over Labrador.

As our guests wandered away into the early dawn Phillip turned to me; 'You fellas ought to come round to Griguet,' he said. 'There's fuel, water, kids for your little one to play with, and the harbour's safe in all weathers. This place now,' he peered at the reddening sky, and shook his head, 'awful bad in a north-easter!'

At ten-thirty the same morning we rolled out of our bunks to a breakfast of codfish steaks supplied by the schoonermen. The weather, flying in the face of the grim prophets of the day before, was not howling out of the north-east but was clear and sharp with a gentle north-west breeze. The Coast of Labrador could be seen in detail at a range of thirty miles.

As we were piling up the dishes Phillip Bridger rumbled down the track in his disreputable pick-up truck, coming to rest with a backfire like a twelve-bore. All hands scrambled aboard to go to the l'Anse aux Meadows site five miles away. As we bounced along, the terrain didn't look remotely like the saga descriptions of Vinland, or even the country around Straumfjord.

'Where's all the hardwood trees?' asked Mike, 'and what about the wild grapes? I know the climate's gone down the tube in the last thousand years, but this place doesn't look much better than Iceland.'

'Actually,' said John, hanging on tight as Phillip skilfully negotiated a gigantic pot-hole, 'it only takes a few degrees of temperature to make a tremendous difference. It's been proved beyond doubt that all those things could easily have been growing here in Eirik the Red's day.'

'Whether they were or not,' interrupted Chris, 'here we are!' As the truck bumped around a corner the surprising sight of two turf longhouses came into view down by the seashore.

'They've weathered well!' said Mike sardonically.

'They're brand new, that's why,' Chris said. 'It seems that they're replicas of the old ones. They've built them beside the foundations of the originals.'

Phillip stopped the truck and we all jumped down. Mike and John came with Ros and myself as we tentatively approached the green mounds and ditches that marked the end of our journey. Chris and Pat, who had already visited them, headed with Hannah towards the strange halls of turf, where grass rustled on the roofs.

Wandering among the deserted moss-covered remains of the Norse winter encampment which form the only tangible evidence that a Viking ever came to Vinland, we four remained silent as our minds free-wheeled down the centuries. After a while I found myself standing beside John. Together we gazed out along the Strait of Belle Isle towards the Atlantic where the blue sea was beginning to fleck with whitecaps as the tide turned.

'I think,' said my old shipmate slowly as though the idea was still taking shape in his mind, 'I understand now why no Norse leader ever sailed twice to Vinland.'

'Why's that?' I asked. I, too, had been thinking of Karlsefni, Freydis, Leif and the rest.

'Because however desirable a place you find when you get here, no-one — not even a hard-case Viking — would ever want to repeat a voyage like that one!'

(overleaf) The 'new' turf longhouse at l'Anse aux Meadows, the only excavated Norse site in North America

Acknowledgements

In writing the 'Norse' part of this book I have drawn extensively on various Icelandic sagas translated into English. Those I have used most are *Eirik the Red Saga, The Greenlanders Saga, Landnamabok, Thorfinn Karlsefni Saga, The Short Saga* and *Njal's Saga*. I am greatly indebted to the published work of Magnus Magnusson, Herman Pálsson and Professor Gwyn Jones for their translations and commentaries, and also to Farley Mowat whose book *Westviking* provided me with a great deal of food for thought.

While *Hirta*'s voyage was at the planning stage, I was given invaluable assistance on the probable weather and ice conditions by the British Meteorological Office at Bracknell. The Icelandic Weather Office, and particularly Dr Thor Jakobsson, gave unstingily of their time and expertise, to say nothing of some enjoyable lunches. These meteorologists played a significant part in the safety of the venture and I am grateful to them all.

To friends in Norway and Iceland, some who appear in the book, others who do not, and who cannot all be named, I wish to record my thanks. Steinar Jørs of Eivindvik would fire anybody's enthusiasm to learn more about the Vikings, and he certainly put a new and living perspective into my own interest. In Newfoundland we received a welcome that was second to none. The hospitality and friendship offered by the folk of Griguet was an experience in human quality that is becoming rare indeed for late-twentieth-century man. To the Bridger family – John, Calip, Phillip and the rest – and to all their friends we owe a debt of thanks. Also to Steve Knudsen, whose perceptive conversation helped stimulate the writing of this book.

Finally the crew, John Lovell, Patrick Green, Chris Stewart, Mike Barker and Gillie McEwan. I can only say that I hope the story does them the justice they all richly deserve. They were chosen with care, they all agreed at once to sign on, and their toughness and long-suffering good humour kept us all afloat.

And of course, Ros, my wife, who did most of the work . . .

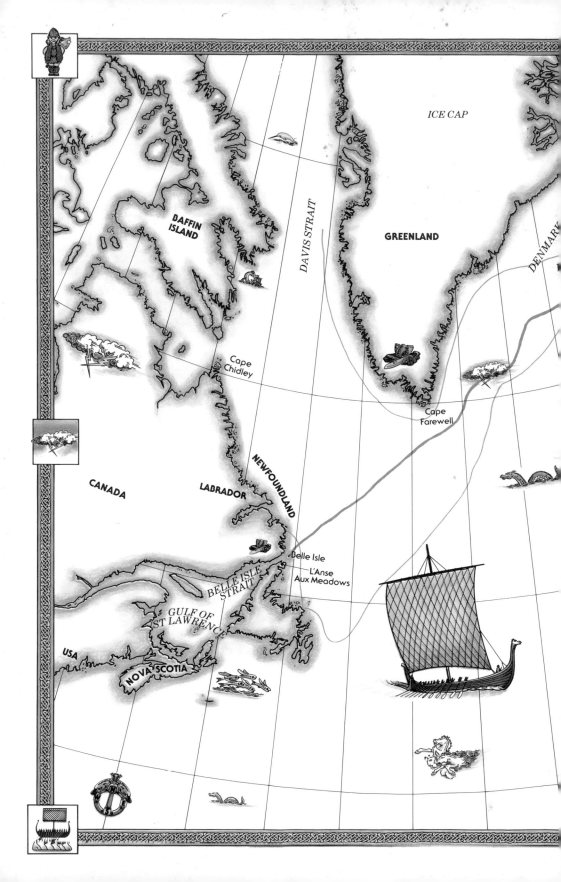

ICE CAP

DAFFIN ISLAND

DAVIS STRAIT

GREENLAND

DENMARK

Cape Chidley

Cape Farewell

CANADA

LABRADOR

NEWFOUNDLAND

Belle Isle

L'Anse Aux Meadows

BELLE ISLE STRAIT

GULF OF ST LAWRENCE

USA

NOVA SCOTIA